Dad, Happy B. ||| | // | '

2007 — Happy

Ashley a Neil
xxx .

LEGEND — SIXTY YEARS AT IBROX

C000214304

RANGERS LEGENDS

BOB McPHAIL

BOB McPHAIL with ALLAN HERRON

MAINSTREAM
PUBLISHING

EDINBURGH AND LONDON

This edition produced exclusively for
Rangers Football Club

First published in Great Britain in 1988 by
MAINSTREAM PUBLISHING COMPANY (EDINBURGH) LTD
7 Albany Street
Edinburgh EH1 3UG

This edition produced exclusively for Rangers Football Club 2001

ISBN 1 84018 541 4

A catalogue record for this book is available from the British Library

Printed and bound in Great Britain by
Cox and Wyman Ltd

For Eleanor and Robbie

Bob McPhail, still full of life at the age of 82, as managing director of his electrical supply company McPhail and Meikle. "I'm really just the oldest message boy in town," he'll tell you.

Acknowledgements

Our grateful thanks go to the *Sunday Mail*, *Daily Record*, *Evening Times*, *Glasgow Herald*, George Outram and D.C. Thomson for the use of the photographs in this book.

Contents

FOUNDED 1873

TELEPHONE
IBROX 159

TELEGRAMS
IBROX PARK
GLASGOW

W. R. SIMPSON. C.A.
SECRETARY

WT STRUTH
MANAGER

THE RANGERS FOOTBALL CLUB LTD
REGISTERED OFFICE:
IBROX PARK · GLASGOW · S·W·1

28th April,1939.

Mr.R.McPhail,
"Lomond",
Etive Drive,
Giffnock,
Glasgow.

Dear Bob,

I am instructed by my Board to confirm offer made
to you for renewal of your contract for season 1939-40,
namely, to pay you the sum of Six Pounds (£6) per week
in Close Season; Six Pounds (£6) per week in Playing; to
be increased to Eight Pounds (£8) per week when playing in
league Team: with bonuses for results.

I shall be glad to have your acceptance of above offer.

Yours faithfully,

Manager.

This was the last contract I was offered — and accepted — by Rangers manager Bill Struth. It states that I would be paid £6 a week during the close season and £8 a week when I played in the first team, with bonuses (£1 for a draw and £2 for a win in league matches) for results.

Twelve years earlier I was given the same contract when I was transferred from Airdrie! I had no complaints. Though I never ever got a rise, and never got a signing-on fee at any time in my career, this was big money in my time. Rangers never scrimped in the treatment of their players — didn't we lap up the luxury of the Turnberry Hotel regularly every season? — and no matter where we travelled, we lived in the best places and always ate the best of food. Struth treated every player equally. We all had the same contract, so we had nothing to argue about. We were well off, and we knew it. So did Bill Struth.

1

When Meiklejohn Buried a Scottish Cup Bogey

I just knew the bogey was about to be buried when our skipper Davie Meiklejohn lined up the penalty kick in the 56th minute. Rangers were about to emerge from a Scottish Cup wilderness that had spanned a frustrating 25 years.

There was never any doubt about the penalty decision. Motherwell referee Willie Bell almost buried his finger on the spot after the Celtic skipper Willie McStay had punched away a shot from our centre-forward, Jimmy Fleming, which had beaten John Thomson. Frankly I thought the ball was fractionally over the line before McStay got his hand to the ball. So did Meiklejohn. He claimed a goal, the referee consulted a linesman, but the penalty decision stood.

It was 24 April, 1928, and a world record crowd of 118,115 for any club match at that time was packed into Hampden, with thousands locked outside. The gates had been closed ten minutes before the kick-off, over 50 people had been injured in the crush to get in and there had been a very real threat of those locked outside rushing the gates. It was the first Scottish Cup final between the "Old Firm" clubs since 1909 when the Cup had been withheld, after two draws, because of a crowd riot. Little did I think, nor indeed did anyone else, that it would be 1953 before the Glasgow giants would meet again in the Scottish Cup, a fourth-round tie which Rangers won 2-0 at Ibrox.

There was a strange silence when "Meek" put the ball on the spot. Seconds later he had driven it powerfully past Thomson's right side and into the back of the net. A well-taken kick. Later I was told the goal had been scored at exactly 4.01 p.m. It must still rank as the most important penalty kick ever taken by a Rangers player. If our skipper had missed then Celtic would have won that final. Not one Rangers player on the field believed otherwise. But there was a calm confidence

11

in the way "Meek" set about taking the kick. He didn't confer with anyone. It was his responsibility as team captain on that day to take it.

In those days at Ibrox when you were given the job of taking penalties, you kept taking them until you missed. It was then the turn of someone else. It just so happens that prior to this Hampden final I had scored three or four in a row . . . and then I missed one. It proved to be a good bit of timing on my part! I would have hated to take *that* kick.

Mind you, I was one of the few who didn't look away when "Meek" stuck the ball in the net. I stood close to our skipper before he ran up to the ball just in case it did happen to come back off the Celtic 'keeper.

Someone said to "Meek" after the match: "You looked like an icicle out there when you took the kick." He replied: "I never felt more nervous in all my life. I just didn't have time to think what it might have meant if I had missed it."

That goal was just the boost we needed. In the 66th minute I got the second goal. It wasn't one of the game's classics. I kicked it over the line from about two yards.

The cross had come from our right-winger, Sandy Archibald, into a crowded goal area. Thomson, under a fair bit of pressure, slightly misjudged the flight of the ball, and I just found myself in the right place at the right time when the ball dropped. As the rest of the lads ran over to congratulate me, Jimmy Fleming, who had a bit of a stutter, said: "B-B-Bob, you t-t-took the b-b-ball right off my toe." I replied: "OK — but it's safer where it is!"

Two minutes later Archibald scored a third goal with a tremendous shot from 25 yards and ten minutes from the end scored again, when he picked up a rebound from a Willie McStay-Jimmy Fleming encounter and smashed the ball with considerable power past Thomson. Again from 25 yards. Victory was ours, by 4-0. The Scottish Cup bogey had been laid to rest. The waiting days were over.

My winning bonus was £20. It just so happens that one of my regular companions on the train from Barrhead to Glasgow each day was the Celtic inside-left Tommy McInally. When I told him what our bonus had been he said: "You didnae win the Cup, Bob, you bought it!"

Celtic of course, were the great cup-fighters. They were the cup-holders on that day and had given us a lot of anxious moments in the goal-less first half when our 'keeper, Tom Hamilton, had to make the save of the match. Midway through the half their right-winger, Pat Connolly, hit the ball on the drop. It looked a scorer all the way but "The Drummer", as Hamilton was known, for reasons I never did find

Celtic inside-forward Alex Thomson watches with some relief as 'keeper John Thomson gets his finger-tips to an awkward cross-ball during the 1928 Scottish Cup final at Hampden. The Rangers predators keeping their eyes on the ball are me, Jimmy Fleming and Andy Cunningham.

out, kept the ball out with a dive that sent the ball to the edge of the box.

Wee Adam McLean, the Celtic left-winger, must have been as surprised at the save as Connolly was, because he scooped the ball over the crossbar. Hamilton, who came from Renfrew, had a dry sense of humour and often complained about not getting enough work to do in his goal. After one match we had won with some ease, he came into the dressing-room with a good old-fashioned dose of the sniffles. "Feeling the cold, Tam?" I asked. He grunted: "Cold? It's no' a goalkeeper Rangers want, it's a policeman."

That long-awaited Scottish Cup win for Rangers put an end to a dressing-room comedy routine which our right-half Jock Buchanan and I used regularly at Ibrox. I had already won a Scottish Cup medal with Airdrie four years earlier and Jock had won a medal with Morton in 1922 in one of the five finals Rangers had lost since their 1903 win over Hearts. Our medals were worn, with the pride of youth, on our watch chain which was, of course, appropriately dangling from the slit pockets of our waistcoats. When we went into the Rangers dressing-room I'd say to Jock: "What's that on your chain there?" He'd reply: "This is my Scottish Cup medal, Bob. What's that on your chain?" I'd make a pretence of examining my medal and say: "Why this is my Scottish Cup medal, Jock."

The Rangers players were not amused by this childish comedy routine. Particularly Davie Meiklejohn and big Andy Cunningham, our inside-right, who had joined the club from Kilmarnock back in 1915 and looked like finishing his career without a winner's medal. He would growl and gripe and make the kind of remarks I won't repeat here, because my grandchildren won't understand them.

Why Jock and I were never physically silenced says much for the dressing-room discipline laid down by manager Bill Struth.

The teams on that unforgettable day were: *Rangers*: T. Hamilton; Gray and R. Hamilton; Buchanan, Meiklejohn, Craig; Archibald, Cunningham, Fleming, McPhail and Morton. *Celtic*: Thomson; W. McStay, Donoghue; Wilson, J. McStay, McFarlane; Connolly, A. Thomson, McGrory, McInally and McLean.

So Andy got his Scottish Cup medal at the age of 37. Would he have played if Tommy Muirhead had been fit? I just don't know. Muirhead, who was the club captain, had been struggling with injury all season and had had a cartilage removed from his knee. Though his recognised position was left-half, he was such a graceful and clever footballer he was every bit at home as an inside-forward. Tommy watched the game from the stand, and never did win a Scottish Cup medal. But that's another story.

Cunningham, a natural left-footed player, and easily recognisable because of his sandy hair, seemed to achieve everything late in his football life. He got his first Scotland cap at the age of 29, and was transferred to Newcastle United the season after our belated Cup win for £2,500. I think he is still in the record book as the oldest débutant in English League football, at the age of 38. Come to think of it, maybe it was his age that made him so crusty at Ibrox!

It was a marvellous moment for me to win a medal with Rangers in my first season with the club, and for Jock Buchanan who had been transferred to Rangers just five months earlier. But there is no way I can put in print the feelings and emotions of the rest of the Rangers team. Players like Cunningham, Sandy Archibald, Davie Meiklejohn, Alan Morton, Tully Craig and Tom Hamilton, who were the experienced members of our team, were beginning to believe in the Cup hoodoo. To produce such a convincing win over Celtic before such an enormous crowd was maybe the peak of their great careers. There might even have been a tear here and there when the referee's whistle was heard for the last time.

I thought the final belonged to Archibald. He took full advantage of the inexperience of the Celtic left-back John Donoghue, who had been pitchforked into the match at the last minute because of an injury to Willie "Peter" McGonagle. Sandy, who came from Crossgates in Fife, had joined Rangers from Raith Rovers in 1917. His crosses, as I soon learned, were something else. He didn't cross the ball, he shot it into the penalty area like a cannonball. You really had to think twice about making contact with your head. If you didn't get it right you had a sore head for a long time after.

What a contrast to the artistic, calculated lobs from wee Alan Morton on the left. Sandy was a strongly built player with a lot of pace, and his two spectacular goals in that final proved just how hard he could hit a ball. He made his own history with Rangers, winning a record 13 championship medals with the club, later equalled by Davie Meiklejohn. He was my team-mate for seven seasons.

Celtic had won the Scottish Cup nine times during the 25 years of Ibrox frustration, so I have to emphasise how very precious this victory was to all those connected with Rangers Football Club. It seemed to me that some great malevolent shadow had been removed from the club.

Celtic couldn't have been more gracious in defeat. There were ready handshakes and smiles for all of us. I recall the Celtic chairman, Tom White, giving the Rangers players a smile when he said to our chairman, Bailie Joseph Buchanan: "I was very glad to have lived long enough to see you lift the Scottish Cup! We at Parkhead are delighted that Rangers have won it. It is their turn." The man meant every word. He knew how much the occasion meant to Rangers.

So here I was, at the age of 22, with two Scottish Cup medals. With my brother Malcolm, winning a medal with Kilmarnock in 1920, the McPhails of Barrhead were doing rather well.

I had joined Rangers on 18 April the previous year. My transfer fee from Airdrie to Rangers, I understand, was £4,500 and my wages were £8 a week in the first team with £2 for a win and £1 for a draw. I'd drop to £6 a week if and when I was in the reserves. Now this was big money in those days. I was told we were the highest-paid players in British football, fractionally ahead of Celtic.

I had had a good final season with Airdrie, scoring 33 goals in 31 league games and had been given my first Scotland cap against England at Hampden just 16 days before. I knew that the Rangers chief scout Alex Young had been watching me — but so had Everton's Scottish scout Jimmy Logan. However I have to say that I was perfectly happy at Airdrie. I had no wish to leave Broomfield. But for some reason that I never had explained to me I was suddenly put on Airdrie's transfer list and this information was circulated to English and Scottish clubs. Did Airdrie really need the money from any transfer? After all they had got £6,500 from Newcastle for Hughie Gallacher just over three years earlier.

Well it seemed that the interest in my future was not confined to Rangers and Everton. I was suddenly involved in a series of interviews with well-dressed gentlemen in Glasgow's St Enoch Hotel. Clubs like Aston Villa, Clapton Orient, Fulham and Derby County spoke to me at great length.

During all the speculation about my future Airdrie took on a friendly fixture with Derby at their Baseball Ground. There was a dinner after the game and while some of the later speeches were in progress I was approached by a waiter who told me that someone wanted to speak to me outside. I left the dining area, and was taken to a room where I was confronted by four men I hadn't seen before. One of them put a key in the door lock and turned it, then told me I wouldn't be allowed to leave the room until I signed for Derby County! It was a bit frightening, but I managed to keep my nerve and assure the gentlemen that I *had* decided to join Derby, but I still had one or two little problems to iron out with Airdrie. This got me off the hook. They accepted what I said with smiles all round and allowed me back to the dining-room. Derby County would be the last club I would sign for!

When I returned to Scotland I then got another shock. I had been left out of the Airdrie team to play Kilmarnock at Rugby Park in a league match. It appeared the Broomfield directors didn't want to risk me getting injured while transfer negotiations were at a delicate stage.

However, through my brother Malcolm, who had played with Kilmarnock, I learned that Airdrie were letting it be known that I was being transferred to Everton on Tuesday "for a handsome sum". My interview with Everton on the Tuesday lasted for a couple of minutes. No way was I going to England.

It was now becoming a real circus as Airdrie had now invited sealed offers for my transfers, which would be opened simultaneously on a

The Rangers team that ended the 25-year-old Scottish Cup hoodoo, by beating Celtic 4-0 in the 1928 final at Hampden Park. With our directors in the background the players are middle row: (left to right) Sandy Archibald, Jimmy Fleming, Davie Meiklejohn, Tom Hamilton, Andy Cunningham, Bob Hamilton and Jock Buchanan. Front: Manager Bill Struth, Dougie Gray, Tully Craig, Tommy Muirhead, who didn't play because of injury, Bob McPhail, Alan Morton and trainer Jimmy Kerr.

given date at Broomfield. I wanted no part of it, and when the date of the sealed offers arrived I phoned to say I wouldn't make it, as I was indisposed.

A week later I was in Glasgow's Kenilworth Hotel to meet Bill Struth and sign for Rangers. It went through so smoothly I wondered what all the fuss had been in the preceding weeks.

Most people had been advising me to do nothing until I spoke to the Rangers manager, Bill Struth. And the advisers included my mother, who didn't want to see her youngest son leave home and live in England. She just couldn't bear the thought of it.

17

Though I had gone through the charade of speaking to a number of English clubs I don't think there was any real doubt in my mind that the club I would join would be Rangers. I got £600 from Airdrie, which was service payment, working out at £150 for each year I had been at Broomfield. The Airdrie directors were the kind of men who did everything by the book, so there was never any question of me getting a few pounds extra on the side. But I did get a "signing on" fee from Rangers. Was it to buy a new bowler hat, black shoes or navy blue suit? I can't remember. But young McPhail suddenly had a lot of money in his pocket. It was a good feeling.

I had been bought by Rangers to replace Tommy Cairns, who had been at Ibrox since 1913, and was their longest-serving player. Cairns knew why I was there. When I was taken into the dressing-room to meet my new team-mates Cairns said to me: "So you're the young fellow coming to replace me? You'll have a job!" Not exactly the warm welcome I had hoped for. I didn't like Cairns too much.

I knew the Rangers players, of course, having played against them during the four seasons I had been with Airdrie and, as I told them at the time, I had the stud marks to prove it. I had also played alongside Cunningham and Morton in a Scotland jersey against England earlier that month. Some time later, in fact, I began to wonder if my new wing partner Alan Morton had exerted any influence in my move to Ibrox. Wee Alan was an Airdrie man, who talked to the people of Airdrie every day of his life, so he knew what was happening at Broomfield. Did he suggest to Struth that I was the youngster who should replace Cairns, who had been his partner for some seven seasons? I wonder!

If I didn't get an enthusiastic welcome from Cairns, my new manager Bill Struth made up for it. After signing for the club, he shook my hand and said: "Young man, you are now with a big club. I wish you the best of luck." I had signed the forms in a restaurant in Glasgow's city centre. Struth drove me from there to Ibrox in his own car. I do recall that I had known better drivers.

The rules of football didn't allow me to turn out in the few remaining league fixtures that Rangers had still to fulfil, so I played myself in with one reserve match and three Charity Cup ties.

The discipline of Struth, a former professional runner who stepped up from club trainer to manager in 1920, was soon apparent. I *was* with a big club. He "suggested" you dress well — black shoes, navy suit, white shirt, appropriate tie, and you would wear a bowler hat on match days.

I'm off and running after scoring Rangers second goal in the 1928 Scottish Cup final at Hampden Park leaving Celtic 'keeper John Thomson lying on the ground looking extremely unhappy.

When we played clubs like Hearts, Hibs, Aberdeen, Raith Rovers and Kilmarnock, Struth insisted that we walk from the railway station to the ground, in order to stretch our legs before the games. He wasn't saving the taxi fares, he really did want us to stretch ourselves after sitting on a train. But he was also applying a fair bit of psychological pressure on the opposition. We must have looked ten foot tall — particularly Cunningham, Tom Hamilton, Bob Hamilton, Davie Meiklejohn, Jock Buchanan and myself, who were the tallest members of the team — as we walked into the various grounds in our heavy coats and bowler hats, looking extremely distinguished and confident. Struth also insisted that when we walked from the stations we should swing our arms. No one was allowed to walk with their hands in their pockets. This did not meet with universal approval among the players, but they did it! Struth would not tolerate untidiness in any shape or form around his beloved Glasgow Rangers.

I enjoyed the training at Ibrox. It was clearly based on the athletic training which Struth had used as a professional runner. In the pre-season at Airdrie, under George Carroll, the emphasis was on sprinting. We did so much work in spiked shoes that our legs would seize up on the way home and we found ourselves hirpling. At Ibrox we had variety, and we didn't seem to work too hard. Running and sprints on a Tuesday, ball work on a Wednesday with the emphasis on passing and control, and loosening up on Thursdays. Friday was the day reserved for a massage and a bath or leisurely shower. During our training we were always conscious of Struth in the stand watching trainer Jimmy Kerr put us through our paces. The man didn't miss much.

In that first season with Rangers I played 45 games for the club and scored 17 goals in 35 league games. I was pleased. I had no great difficulty in settling in. I soon found that most of the players were as greetin'-faced as I was and that Struth encouraged us to bark at each other. "Get the whip out," Struth would command when he thought one or two were slacking a bit. There was never any great tactical advice from the man. His pre-match speech was much the same week after week: "Now then, you've a job to do. Go out and do it."

Wee Alan Morton soon let me know what he expected of me. In an early game I floated a lobbed pass over a defender's head to the wee fellow out on the bye-line. He made no effort to stop the ball with his head. I shouted: "Why didn't you get it with your head?" He glared and shouted back: "Look Bobby, the name of the game is *foot*ball — and it is played on the ground."

Wee Alan didn't like to get his hair messed up. He had rather a neat parting in his glossy black hair and he just didn't fancy getting it dirtied. Over the years I played with him I think I could count on one hand the number of times he headed the ball. I learned to give him the ball at his feet, or in front of him. For a wee man he had a deep voice and to this very day I can hear that unmistakable voice shouting: "Right Bobby." and then he'd be off, haring down the wing, waiting for my pass . . . to his feet.

Seven days after winning that historic Scottish Cup final, Rangers fielded the same team against Kilmarnock at Ibrox to clinch the League

Celtic's skipper Willie McStay keeps his eye on 'keeper John Thomson as he cuts out an Alan Morton cross during the 1928 Scottish Cup final. That's me on the left, ready to take advantage of any defensive slip-up.

Championship. We beat them 5-1, Jimmy Fleming scored a hat-trick and the ageless Andy Cunningham scored twice. We finished five points ahead of Celtic to retain the championship, and I found myself with a league and cup double in my first season. Fleming had proved himself a prolific scorer in the league with 35 goals in 35 games.

Our Cup run to Hampden had been reasonably smooth. Rangers lost just three goals in the six games. We beat East Stirling 6-0, Cowdenbeath 4-2, King's Park 3-1, had a wee bit of a struggle to beat Albion Rovers 1-0 at Coatbridge, and beat Hibs 3-0 in the semi-final at Tynecastle, where a sporting journalist described me thus: "McPhail had all the makings of a rugby player in his dealings with Robb." He was referring to Willie Robb in the Hibs goal, who had played previously with Rangers. I think I remember bumping into Willie once or twice in going for a ball!

Came Hampden and the barren years were over. The bogey was laid to rest. But I have a tailpiece to add.

On 5 May of that season we met Celtic in the semi-final of the Glasgow Charity Cup at Ibrox. And the 27,000 crowd were given a re-run of that legendary Cup final penalty incident. Midway through the second half Sandy Archibald beat John Thomson with a shot so typical of our winger, and there was Willie McStay, the Celtic skipper, to punch the ball over the crossbar! A penalty. This time there was no Davie Meiklejohn to take it. He was out with an injury. His replacement at centre-half was big Bob Ireland from Darvel. Step forward McPhail!

While at Airdrie our 'keeper Jock Ewart used to tell me that, when taking a penalty kick, I should aim at the iron stanchion holding up the net at the back of the goal, to the left side of the 'keeper. "Hit it hard and accurately and you'll score every time," he would say. For the most part I did. But while most 'keepers are reckoned to be daft, they are not stupid, and some remembered where I would try to place the kick. John Thomson certainly remembered, because he got his hands to my kick and pushed it on to the crossbar. Fortunately for me the ball came back out again, and I managed to hit the rebound past him. Jimmy Fleming scored in the last minute in a 2-0 win, and we went on to beat Queen's Park 2-1 in the final.

I felt the country boy from Barrhead had done well among the great names of Rangers at Ibrox in his first season. How was I to know things would only get better?

2

When Four in a Bed was a Way of Life

As the seventh son in a family of ten, I suppose you could say I was born into a football team. I arrived on 25 October, 1905, in a two-storey tenement property called "big Dealston" in Paisley Road, Barrhead, the ninth child of Elizabeth and Malcolm McPhail. My wee sister Bessie had still to arrive.

My dad was head gardener with the local Fulton family who owned the Glenfield Works near Barrhead. I recall him with nothing but affection. He was a church elder who respected the Sabbath and saw nothing but good in people. He regarded his family with wholesome pride and, I recall with some embarrassment, he was still cutting my hair when I became a professional footballer with Airdrie.

I don't think I ever saw my mother sit down or even get the chance to fall asleep in a chair in my life. She was always working. She always seemed to be cooking, sewing, mending, cleaning up or baking. Though, as I recall, her soda scones rarely ever got the chance to cool down before they were eaten. To this day I remember sticking holes in her hot soda scones, putting margarine into the holes, and then woolfing them down.

Spoiled? I don't think so. But with six big brothers and two elder sisters, Maggie and Nellie, to look after me, I was never short of a bit of protection on the playground at Grahamston School or on the streets where I first kicked a tanner ba'. On the occasions I was invited to the rear of the school at four o'clock to sort out a particular problem with some protagonist, my brother Tommy, who was a couple of years older than me, would take my place. So I didn't get too many bloodied noses!

If we were poor, we didn't know it, because we were one big happy family. The seven boys would share two beds. I slept four in a bed — two at the top and two at the bottom, and I got more kicks while I was sleeping than I ever got playing football. Many a time I was kicked out of bed. I can recall, quite vividly, wakening one night to find myself under the bed with the room in complete darkness. I was terrified. I was scared to move a muscle, never mind return to bed, as I was convinced "the bogey man" was waiting to grab me.

Meals were a bit hectic with plenty of porridge in the morning, as the old-fashioned sustainer, and saps — a mixture of bread, margarine and boiled milk — at night for dinner. There was always plenty of bread and cakes on the table. My dad would always eat a cake before eating bread. He would say: "If I don't get a cake now, I never will." He was right.

The McPhails always went to Saltcoats for a summer holiday. The train direct from Barrhead to the Ayrshire coast. The distance was a mere 33 miles, but to me it was another world, of sun, sand and salt water. It couldn't have been much of a break for my poor mother. She still had to clean the house we rented and make all the meals, but I never heard her complaining.

When I hear the young people of today say they are bored and can't find anything to do, I despair. The days were never long enough for the kids in Barrhead. Whatever happened to the boys who stood for ages, heading a ball against a tenement building, trying to improve a personal record of "keepy-up"? I now only have memories of those who would throw down their pullover and jacket as goalposts, and challenge their school chum to a "heiders" competition. First to score three goals signalled half-time. First to score six was the winner. "Heiders" kept your shoes clean and avoided you getting a hiding from your mother.

I've just told you why there were so many brilliant headers of the ball in the game in my day. If someone produced a ball on a nearby street or a piece of wasteground, in no time there would be a game. We'd play until we dropped or it got dark.

Life in Barrhead had nothing but good memories. I attended Barrhead Bourock Church, where I was a member of the 2nd Barrhead Boy's Brigade company. As this was the period of the 1914-18 war, we did all our drills with wooden rifles. The discipline of the BB stood me in good stead as a player and as a person.

Mind you, I was no angel. I have to confess with some shame that I was smoking that early. In those days you could buy a packet of five "Woodbines" for a penny. For a ha'penny you could buy two "Woodbines". Why did we smoke so young? Because the rest of the kids did it. Stupid, wasn't it?

The McPhail family of Barrhead in all its finery gathered in a "team" group my mother had some difficulty in organising, and treasured so much. Back row: (left to right) Jimmy, Maggie, John and Malcolm, who won a Scottish Cup medal with Kilmarnock. Front: Father, Tommy, Hugh, Willie, me, Nellie and Mother. Bessie had still to arrive. How I hated those button boots!

My mother was horrified when she found out my secret vice. She had got so concerned as to why I didn't seem to be growing that she sent for the doctor, whose name was Corbett. As this gentleman had a wooden leg, he was known affectionately in the district as "Pinny". The doctor's first question to me just about shattered my mother. "Well, how many cigarettes have you had today?" The Doc was no fool! It then came out that I had been seen picking up "dog ends" in the street, sticking a pin in them, and puffing them. Right there and then I was due the hiding of a lifetime but Bessie, the youngest of the family, pleaded with my mother that I had learned my lesson — and I got away with it. Bessie was to prove a good ally to me throughout my life.

If I wasn't spoiled at home, then I think I might have been a wee bit privileged. I was the only one who ever got new football boots. I just couldn't look up for looking down at these brand new boots on my feet, with the thick new laces. Boy, did I take care of them! No way would I play in the streets with these boots. It would have worn away the leather studs. They were worn only for games on the grass. I used to clean them, polish them and hide them away. They were mine.

When you are the youngest of seven sons you have no problems getting clothes. You inherit those of your brothers. I wore nothing but hand-me-downs. But didn't every family in those days? Parents simply couldn't afford to buy new clothes for the big families of the time. Someone, somewhere had made a big sacrifice to buy me new boots. Was it a birthday present? Was it a Christmas present? I have to admit that I don't remember where they came from, but they were my proudest possession.

The first real influence of my footballing life was my science teacher at Barrhead High School, Davie Wilson. He looked after the football teams and on his recommendation I was chosen to play in the international schoolboy trials for under-14s on a ground near Glasgow's Eglinton Toll. This man offered me nothing but encouragement from the first time I met him. I think he was more delighted than I was when I got my first international cap at the age of 13 against Wales at Vetch Field Park, Swansea. In the trials I scored a goal and must have made an impression as an inside-left. So off went young McPhail to visit his first foreign country — Wales. The big time beckoned!

It was the first time I had ever travelled on a corridor train. I just couldn't sit at peace all the way south from Glasgow, marvelling at the changing countryside through the windows and travelling at what I then considered the remarkable speed of 60 mph. Lunch on a train at the age of 13? I was having delusions of grandeur.

So on 3 March, 1919, I wore the colours of Scotland for the first time. Scotland's team: Wilkie (John Street); Allan (Wellshot), Blair (Whitehill); McLachlan (Larbert), Drummond (Bellahouston), Coyle (St. Aloysius); McKenzie (Clydebank), Hislop (Whitehill), Lithgow (Hutcheson's), McPhail (Barrhead), Marshall (Hutcheson's). We won 2-0 and I scored the second goal.

Unfortunately, there had to be a change for the match with England at Hampden a week later. It was discovered that our left-back, Danny Blair from Whitehill Secondary, had been "plunking" school. He was immediately dropped for the England match, as punishment. He must have been heart-broken. Imagine missing a go at the "Auld Enemy" because you had dodged school for a couple of days? Did no one have the understanding of Mr. Chips in these days?

By a strange twist of fate, or fortune, the next time I was to play in the same team as Danny was against Wales. This time in a full international nine years later at Ibrox when Scotland won 4-2 with Hughie Gallacher scoring a hat-trick. By this time Danny was playing with Clyde and I was with Rangers.

Three years later Blair did play against England. We were both in the Scotland team at Hampden that won 2-0 before a crowd of 129,810. Danny and Joe Nibloe of Kilmarnock were the Scottish full-backs. Our scorers that day were George Stevenson of Motherwell and Jimmy McGrory of Celtic. I think this occasion more than made up for his misfortune in 1919. Danny, who moved on to Aston Villa, played eight times in all for Scotland. He was an outstanding full-back in a period when every back in the country looked good enough to play for Scotland.

The boy who replaced Danny in that schoolboy match with England was George Stirling, who had been the reserve in Wales. I recall his name because he lived up the same close as the McPhails in Barrhead. He was actually a left-winger, but fitted in easily at full-back.

Prior to this match, which was watched by 17,000, we were all surprised when a little man, extremely dapper and wearing a bowler hat, came into the Hampden dressing-room to wish us all the best. Because I was the smallest boy in the team — was it really the dreaded "Woodbines"? — this mysterious little man with the long stride got his eye on me. He walked over briskly, touched me on the shoulder, and said: "Good luck, boy." When he had gone, one of the boys said with some awe: "Do you know who that was?" I replied that I did not. "That was Alan Morton!"

At that time Morton was playing with Queen's Park. Little did he think that I would be his partner in so many great Rangers triumphs in the not too distant future. By the time I joined Rangers I stood five feet ten and a half inches, so it wasn't easy to convince Alan that the wee laddie he had spoken to at Hampden back in 1919 was yours truly.

I think I should mention that we hammered England 5-0 and I remember our big centre-half, George Drummond of Bellahouston Academy, almost bursting the net with two right-foot shots. The gate receipts that day were £464.2s.10d. At that time it was 6d to watch this match, 8d to watch a senior game, and a penny to buy a morning paper.

The gold medal I got for playing in both these internationals is still the most prized posession I have from my football career. I wouldn't swap it for any of my seven Scottish Cup medals or nine championship medals. Why not? I find that difficult to explain. Because it was the first tangible success I had in football? Or maybe it is the constant reminder of the day a dream came true for a 13-year-old boy from Barrhead. I'm not really sure.

Suddenly my school days were over at the age of 14. I was now a delivery boy with Galbraith's, the local grocery shop. I delivered everything the hard way, by foot, and in a basket that threatened to pull my arms from their sockets.

Very early I learned that good service could be financially beneficial. I remember that the best tips to be had were at Nitshill, which linked Barrhead and Glasgow, and was where the miners stayed. Some tipped as much as threepence. A penny tip was normal. The minister at Levern Church, the Rev. Thomas Cook, was a generous man, so long as you didn't break any of his eggs. He got my services on a Friday when I could expect an apple or a "jelly piece" as a reward.

What my mother didn't know, didn't harm her. So I neglected to tell her about my "additional income". If I had she wouldn't have given me any pocket money, which was generally threepence. I must have been a deceitful child!

It wasn't long before I started playing regularly with Ashvale Juveniles alongside three of my brothers. John was at right-back, Willie was centre-half and Jimmy was the kind of centre-forward who would have run through a brick wall. We played all our matches on the local Cowan Park. Our fiercest rivals were Paisley Carlyle. Some of these games were memorable! A bit of brotherly love and understanding must have paid off because we won the Renfrewshire Juvenile Cup and I still have that medal among my collection today.

I think it was around this time that my father lost his job as head gardener. By this time we were living, rent free, in the cottage of the grounds of the "big house" at Glenfield. Younger members of the Fulton family took over and suddenly my father found himself under a bit of pressure to do work on a Sunday, which he had always steadfastly refused to do because of his Christian beliefs. He had been asked by the new "Madam" to cut fresh flowers each Sunday and lift certain vegetables. This didn't appeal to father, who managed a compromise of doing these chores on a Saturday and keeping them fresh for uplifting the following day. But the crunch came when he was asked to wash the family car one Sunday. My father dug his heels in, pointing out that he was a gardener and not a chauffeur. He was given two months to find new accommodation . . . and a new job.

For a spell we lived in the local manse, which was temporarily vacant. Then, in sheer desperation, we had to live for a period in a single room,

28

My first Scotland cap! The Scottish schoolboys' team which beat Wales 2-0 at Swansea in 1919 and that wee laddie to the right of the back row is me. Team is — Back: McKenzie (Clydebank), Coyle (St Aloysius), Wilkie (John Street), Stirling (Barrhead) who was reserve, and McPhail (Barrhead). Middle: Allan (Wellshot), McLachlan (Larbert), Drummond (Bellahouston, captain), Lithgow (Hutcheson's), and Hislop (Whitehall). Front: Blair (Whitehill), who went on to play with Clyde, Aston Villa and Scotland, and Marshall (Hutcheson's).

offered by my now married brother, Willie. There were eight of us in that room, including my mother and father. It must have been sheer hell for them.

My father didn't have a job and he couldn't find a home. Four of the family were now married, but that must have been the lowest period of my father's life. Eventually we moved to a tenement property in Graham Street and my father found work as a labourer in the local Shanks factory. He was probably earning about £2.10s. a week. I earned more as an 18-year old part-time player with Airdrie.

As a delivery boy I was experiencing some difficulty in getting away on a Saturday afternoon to play football, so I suggested to my father that maybe it was about time I learned a trade. All my brothers were tradesmen, why not me? John was an engineer, Jimmy a painter,

Malcolm — who won a Scottish Cup medal with Kilmarnock in 1920 — was a baker, Willie and Tommy were blacksmiths and Hugh was a grocer.

Now, it so happened that one of our neighbours when we had stayed at Bellfield Street, Tom Bell, was a foreman in the nearby Cochrane's Foundry. He was approached and he said he would see what he could do. Soon I was serving an apprenticeship as a moulder. Mr Bell was an avid Airdrie supporter and when I began playing with Pollok Juniors in Glasgow, he soon had the chief Airdrie scout, Jock Weir, checking me over. I enjoyed my days with the Juniors, and recall the help I got from the club's outside-right, Wallace Lambie. He was very much the father figure to me, making it easy for me to make passes, giving non-stop encouragement and talking me through a game.

We must have had a fair wee team, because we won a cup. I think they called it the Scott Cup. Jock Weir was now a regular visitor to the McPhail home after every Pollok match and was now suggesting it was time I considered becoming a professional footballer — with Airdrie. They were the only senior club to show any real interest in me at this time, and any decision I had to make I had to make alone. I had just turned 18. I just didn't think to consult my father.

I was earning 17/9d a week as an apprentice moulder. When I signed for Airdrie as a part-time professional, I was given a signing fee of £20, the biggest amount of money I had ever seen in my life, and £3 a week in the reserve team. If I ever made the first team then I would get £5 a week and bonuses of 10s. for a draw and £1 for a win.

I signed for Airdrie on Christmas Day, 1923. I was in the big money . . . but it still wasn't time to give up my apprenticeship at the foundry.

3

The Greedy Genius of Hughie Gallacher

I played my first game alongside Hughie Gallacher on 21 March, 1924, a Thursday afternoon, at Ibrox. It was the third replay of a fourth-round Scottish Cup-tie with Ayr United — and I found myself in the Airdrie team at extremely short notice.

I had reported for work as usual in the morning at the Cochrane's Foundry in Barrhead, pursuing my trade as a moulder. But within minutes my whole life-style was to change. My foreman, Tom Bell — the Airdrie supporter who had got me the job — came rushing up to me and said: "Bob, get yourself cleaned up and get to Ibrox. You're playing for Airdrie this afternoon!"

There had been a lot of drama in the Broomfield boardroom of which I knew nothing. During the second replay against Ayr United the previous day, the Airdrie inside-left, Jimmy Howieson, who had a streak of bad temper in his make-up, got himself ordered off near the end of extra time with the score at 1-1. The Airdrie directors virtually decided there and then that Howieson wouldn't play for the club again. Now Jimmy was a good player — an extremely good player — who moved on to St. Mirren and played for Scotland against Northern Ireland three years later in Belfast. The Broomfield board, however, was made up of local dignatories like magistrates, councillors and prominent businessmen who were very concerned with their own image and that of the club. They were furious that an Airdrie player had been sent off because of violent behaviour. So it was decided that Howieson would be dropped, and Bob McPhail would make his first-team debut in an extremely difficult Scottish Cup replay. My days as a moulder were numbered.

I arrived at Ibrox in a bit of a daze and made my way to the old pavilion at the top of what seemed endless steps, to become a member of one of the best teams in Scottish football at that time. What I didn't realise of course was that these were the glory days for Airdrie. They were to finish runners-up four times in a row in the championship from 1923 and of course got their only Scottish Cup win in the year of my debut, 1924.

It was a great feeling to start my full-time career with Airdrie with a win. We beat Ayr United 1-0 in this marathon fourth-round tie, which had taken four games and six and a half hours to decide. Hughie Gallacher got the winner.

"Wee Hughie", as he was affectionately known by Airdrie supporters, was just five feet, five inches tall. He was almost three years older than me, but he had already established himself as one of the finest centre-forwards of his time.

I didn't like him. He was a selfish wee fellow. He thought of no one but himself. He virtually ignored me when I went into the dressing-room that day. I got no words of encouragement from him on that occasion, nor on any other occasion. All that mattered to Hughie was Hughie. He was a superb centre-forward, and he knew it. He had a vicious tongue and he used it on opponents. I learned swear words from Hughie I had never heard before. He was a winner on the field, and if he had to upset his opponents to win, then he wouldn't hesitate to do so.

Gallacher could turn on a penny piece. He wasn't a particularly fast player. Indeed, he could be quite deliberate at times. But he had a superb sense of getting himself into the right position, and was extremely agile when he had to be. He was never caught off balance. He shielded the ball, probably better than any other player I've seen, rode tackles with disdain, using his backside when necessary. He was a clever player, good on the ball.

This wee man who scored a lot of good goals with his head, despite his lack of inches, was a success because he just seemed to know where the ball would land in the box. I remember his fury in one of my early games with Airdrie when I scored with a header from our outside-right, Jimmy Reid, who was old enough to be my father. As I turned towards Gallacher looking for a bit of praise, he snapped: "Hey, that's my job." I surprised myself by replying: "But you weren't there, were you?"

I had to admire the many talents of this rough little diamond of a man, but I could never really take to him as a friend. Even in that first game against Ayr United he was giving the centre-half, Jimmy

McLeod, a really bad time with his tongue. Every time he went near the big fellow he would give him a mouthful. Eventually I said: "Look, Hughie, why don't you leave him alone. He has played you fairly all afternoon." I was told very sharply to mind my own bloody business.

Gallacher was God at Broomfield. He could do no wrong, even in the eyes of the directors, who would never countenance anything untoward, like giving the players an extra few bob on the side if they had a good win. These gentlemen stuck to the terms of your contract like limpets. They were not flexible men. They were so honest it hurt your pocket. If the bonus was £1 for a win, then there was no more.

It has to be said that it was Gallacher's scoring genius in the early round that got Airdrie to their only Scottish Cup win that year. The truth is that they were just nine minutes away from a first-round defeat! It was Gallacher who scored the equaliser against Morton in the 81st minute. Right on the whistle Willie Russell, one of the smoothest-playing inside-forwards I ever saw, got the winner with Hughie lying in the back of the net having missed the cross ball, which Willie didn't. Morton protested furiously that Gallacher was offside. But the goal stood.

In the second round against St. Johnstone, Gallacher scored the first of the four goals in a 4-0 win. In the third round he got two goals in a 5-0 win over Motherwell. Came that fourth-round marathon with Ayr United and it was the man himself who got the equaliser in a 1-1 draw. In the replay he hit the post in a 0-0 draw. It was Russell who scored in the 1-1 draw in the third game and, as I said before, Gallacher got the only goal in the fourth game that Thursday afternoon at Ibrox. He failed to score in the semi-final with Falkirk at Celtic Park where our left-winger, Jimmy Sommerville, who became a golf professional, got our two goals. Englishman Syd Puddefoot got the Falkirk goal.

To his considerable disgust, Hughie didn't score in the final against Hibs where there was a crowd of 59,218. Willie Russell scored both our goals with his head in a 2-0 win. But the terrier-like attitude of Gallacher caused havoc with the Hibs defenders. He and Russell were easily our best forwards.

I have been asked a thousand times if Hughie Gallacher was the best centre-forward I ever saw. I have had to consider this very carefully, but my straight answer now is *no*. Later in this book I'll give you my reasons, but this man certainly was one of the best I ever played with. His very record establishes him as one of the all-time greats. A legend.

During his career Hughie Gallacher scored 541 goals, including

The only Airdrie side ever to win the Scottish Cup, in 1924. Back row: (left to right) Trainer George Carroll, W. Neil, R. McPhail, J. McDougall, J. Ewart, T. Preston, D. Gordon, J. Allan, J. Murdoch, assistant trainer Willie Reid. Front row: J. Sommerville, J. Reid, W. Russell, H. Gallacher, G. McQueen (captain), A. Dick, R. Bennie and J. Howieson.

387 goals on either side of the border. In 20 games for Scotland — if he had got himself sorted out off the field he would have played many, many more games for his country — he scored 24 times, including five in one game against Northern Ireland in Belfast in 1929. He led the famous "Wembley Wizards" attack in 1928 at Wembley, when Scotland won 5-1, but just couldn't get his name on the score sheet.

Hughie was from Bellshill in Lanarkshire, where he played with the local Junior side, Bellshill Athletic. He had a brief period with Queen of the South before joining Airdrie. When he was transferred from Airdrie to Newcastle United just eight months after our Scottish Cup win over Hibs, the transfer fee was a British record £6,500. An enormous amount of money for a club like Airdrie.

The wee man gave value for money. In his first seven games with Newcastle he scored 13 goals. He was an instant idol, and when he helped them win the First Division Championship in 1927 he set a club scoring record of 36 league goals. Maybe if he had stayed on Tyneside his quality of life would have been happier than it turned out. However, argument, confrontation and problems were never far away from Hughie and in 1930 he was on the move again. This time to London, and the bright lights. He was transferred to Chelsea for £10,000. Right then he was at his peak. He was Scotland's regular centre-forward, and from time to time I would meet him on international occasions. He hadn't changed. He was still full of himself, and very conscious of the impact and influence he had on the football public.

Fancy the bunnets? Hughie Gallacher and yours truly look distinctly uncomfortable as we glare at the photographer in the middle of Copenhagen during Airdrie's close-season tour of Scandinavia in 1924.

I'm told that hundreds of Newcastle fans wept when he was transferred to Chelsea. For some it was the end of the world. To the Newcastle public he was the greatest centre-forward that ever lived. When he returned to St. James' Park for the first time as a Chelsea player in September 1930, the crowd was a ground record 63,386. That record still stands today, and will never be beaten, because the ground has been modernised and the capacity reduced. I've never known a greater public tribute to the popularity of any player during my lifetime in football. The Newcastle fans had turned up to see "Wor Hughie" and they applauded him on and off the field. The result didn't matter. It made me realise that I had been playing with a legend at Airdrie and hadn't known it! Had I been too close to him to fully appreciate his genius? Gallacher admitted in later years that the demonstration of sheer adulation from the Newcastle fans had been the most memorable occasion of his life.

London's bright lights were doing Hughie's career no good whatsoever. His international career was virtually over. He made only two further appearances, against England in 1934, his only cap as a Chelsea player; and England again the following year, this time while with Derby County. This restless wee man continued to play until he was 36, moving to Notts County, Grimsby and finally Gateshead, where he settled. I was quite shattered to read that he had ended his own life on 11 June, 1957, by throwing himself in front of a train on the nearby Newcastle-King's Cross line at the age of 54.

He had been charged with ill-treating and assaulting his young son, Matthew, and was due to appear in court the following day. Hughie had become a lonely, tragic figure, struggling to make a living. He lived alone after the death of his wife and had admitted publicly some days before his tragic death: "Drink has been my downfall."

Hughie's contribution to the history of football is immense. On reflection he put much more into the game than he ever got out of it, and the company he kept in London as a Chelsea player did him nothing but harm. But he was never the kind of man who would listen to the advice of those who had his best interests at heart. More's the pity.

I was four years with Airdrie, and thoroughly enjoyed every day I was there. The manager was Willie Orr, a former Celtic half-back who had played three times for Scotland. I was a mere kid when he signed me in Willie Maley's restaurant at the foot of Queen Street in Glasgow. To me he was an awesome figure. He had actually played with Celtic!

Willie was a fine man. He was a great help to me and was always ready to give me any advice I might need. I have nothing but good memories of the man. He had built a good side at Airdrie and had given the town the only major trophy they've ever won — the 1924 Scottish Cup. When he moved to Leicester a year later I missed him badly. The winning team was: Ewart; Dick, McQueen; Preston, McDougall, Bennie; Reid, Russell, Gallacher, McPhail and Sommerville. I was the "babe" at 18 years and six months old.

I seem to recall that Hibs were favourites to win, but within two and a half minutes Airdrie were a goal up and I was involved in the goal. Our right-winger, Jimmy Reid, whose accurate crosses had provided dozens of scoring chances for Hughie Gallacher, had been chosen for sentimental reasons. He had been a long-term servant of the club and Willie Orr and the directors felt he had the right to play in this final even though his best days were over. Hughie might well have had some influence on Jimmy playing, as they had the kind of understanding that Willie Waddell and Willie Thornton had much later with Rangers. It was from Jimmy's corner that I got my head to the ball, instead of Hughie, and sent it across goal. Willie Russell met it and scored. Half an hour later our best player on the day, and the best player in the final, Bob Bennie, lobbed the ball into the Hibs area, and there was Russell to meet it again with his head and beat the Hibs and Scotland 'keeper, Willie Harper, for the second time.

I was certain I had scored just on half-time when I managed to work my way through the Hibs defence and got a full shot on target from well inside the penalty box. I knew then why Harper was Scotland's 'keeper. He not only stopped my shot, he held it. In the end we were good winners. I felt I had played quite well, but there were a lot of experienced players around me.

Bob Bennie, who was at left-half, playing behind me, came from Airdrie and turned on the game of his life. Not surprisingly he went on to gain three Scottish caps. And Jock Ewart, our 'keeper, had been in great form. Ewart, who had played with Bradford City, was a real character. He was always ready for a good dram, so long as someone else bought it.

He took an interest in me, and was always making sure I wasn't being ignored. He once took me out for a bit of shooting practice at Broomfield. He would throw the ball out to me from the goal-line and get me to fire the ball back at him. Eventually he stopped and said to me: "Listen, son. Do you always hit the ball like that?" I asked: "Like what?" He said: "There's a spin in every ball I've tried to hold from you. How are you striking the ball?" As a natural right-footed player, even though I played inside-left, I had been hitting the ball with the outside of my right foot, putting a powerful spin on the ball of which I had never really been aware. Said Jock: "Don't change it. You keep hitting them like that, son, and you'll get a lot of goals. A ball like that is difficult to hold."

I took his advice, for these were the days of the ball that got heavier in the mud and rain and had a lacing, which caused many a gash on a defender's head as he tried to head it away. The slippery ball, hit first time with a spin, could be a goalie's nightmare. Jock had got his only Scotland cap against England in 1921, in a 3-0 win at Hampden. His proud boast was that in all his games for Scotland he had never lost a goal!

Russell, our two-goal match-winner, had got the first of his three Scotland caps against Wales in February. Gallacher had got his first Scotland cap on his 21st birthday on 1 March against Northern Ireland, while Jimmy Reid had been first capped back in 1914 against Wales. So there was a fair bit of quality about this Airdrie team.

Russell, who enjoyed a good dram, like Ewart, was a beautiful player to watch. He had marvellous ball control, would nurse the ball until he was ready to make a pass, and would wait for you to get in position. He could be crabbit when things weren't going right, but he was a tremendous help to Hughie Gallacher. Hughie had a lot to thank him for because Willie took a lot of weight off him. Willie was very much my kind of player.

Our bonus for winning the Scottish Cup was £8 — and not a penny more. Our celebration dinner was held in Rombach's restaurant in Glasgow where our chairman, Hon. Sheriff Tom Forsyth, thanked us for bringing the Cup to Airdrie. Thereafter it was an open-topped bus tour through Airdrie, where thousands lined the streets. Would football always be like this, I wondered?

Four years earlier my brother, Malcolm, had experienced the same thrills when he played on the left wing for the Kilmarnock Cup-winning side against Albion Rovers at Hampden, where a record 95,000 crowd saw Killie win 3-2. Like Airdrie, it was their first Cup win.

I now had a gold medal to put on my Albert chain, worn on the waistcoat, just like my brother. And I had a gold watch to go with it, compliments of Henderson's the Jewellers. That watch is still going to this day!

Even in those days it was have boots, will travel, and I thoroughly enjoyed a close-season tour of Norway and Denmark with Airdrie, during which time our manager, Willie Orr, always concerned with my welfare, drew me aside and told me in all seriousness: "Look, son, Oslo is rotten with venereal disease, so keep away from the wimmin. It's up to yourself, mind you, but a couple of minutes pleasure could become a lifetime of misery." That was enough for me. I haven't the slighest doubts now that there probably wasn't one reported case of VD anywhere in Oslo at that time. But Willie's words convinced me not to do anything that my mother would not approve.

We sailed to Oslo. The first time I have ever been on a ship. I enjoyed it so much I went right up to the bow and leant over to watch the ship plough its way through the heavy swell. I found it exhilarating. The captain of the ship did not. He sent out three blasts on the ship's siren system to get my attention and then shouted: "Get to hell out of there. You'll drown yourself." When I went to tell my team-mates about my experience, I found half of them in their bunks dying of sea-sickness. I was never up nor down.

Though we weren't probably aware of it at the time, Airdrie wasn't quite the same team without Hughie Gallagher. New centre-forwards came and went, but none ever made the same impact as "Wee Hughie".

On 27 April, 1927, I got my one and only cap as an Airdrie player, against England at Hampden Park. I was once again teamed up with Gallacher, who had just had the greatest season of his career with Newcastle. This time the chemistry didn't work. Neither of us got a goal, and we lost 2-1. England's scorer was William Ralph "Dixie" Dean, of Everton, making his international debut. Alan Morton was Scotland's scorer.

Exactly 16 days later, I was a Rangers player.

4

The Day I Refused to Play for Struth

Greta Garbo may have wanted to be alone, but she had company. Me! We got on to the lift together on the ground floor of New York's Knickerbocker Hotel and travelled all the way to the top floor without exchanging a word.

I was 22 years of age — the same age as Garbo — and had arrived in New York with Rangers on their first tour of the United States and Canada in May 1928. For the first time in their history Rangers had just completed a League and Scottish Cup double, beating Celtic by five points for the championship and by four goals in the Scottish Cup final. So we were of good cheer after our journey on the good ship *California* from Greenock to New York.

I have to admit I had no idea who my travelling companion was on the lift. I noted the false eyelashes, the extravagance of red lipstick and her general make-up and thought to myself: "She looks a bit like a painted doll." When the lift doors opened at the top floor, some of my team-mates were waiting. Remembering my manners, I allowed the lady out of the lift first, and was a bit surprised to see the stunned reaction of men like Jock Buchanan, Davie Meiklejohn and Jimmy Fleming. Their conversation ceased as the lady swept past them without giving them the slightest hint of a glance. When I emerged they said: "What did she say to you? What did you say to her?" They couldn't believe it when I said I had ignored her. They then realised I didn't know who my lift companion had been.

"That was Greta Garbo, you idiot!" they shouted, almost in chorus. "Don't tell us you didn't recognise her!" I hadn't. It took me the whole tour to live that one down. How can you travel with the Hollywood love goddess, alone, in the confines of a lift and stand like a dummy and fail to recognise her, or even appreciate her? What would have happened if

I had said: "Good afternoon" or "Are you having a nice time?" or, that great original line, "Haven't we met somewhere before?" My imagination ran away with me for many a long day after that lift journey. It didn't help me any when the fame of this legendary Swedish actress began to spread, and she was four times nominated for Oscars, particularly for her roles in *Camille* and *Ninotchka.* I couldn't even honestly tell my friends I had met the lady. Because I muffed my only chance to speak to her.

Well if I didn't have any success with Miss Garbo I certainly couldn't complain about my achievements with a pair of well-studded boots on my feet. I finished up top scorer on the tour with 14 goals.

It started with a hat-trick in Philadelphia against a National American league select, when manager Bill Struth made it clear that this was going to be no holiday trip. We were here to win every game and play as well as we could. We were representing Rangers and Scotland. He demanded nothing but the best from us, on and off the field. With ten international players — including our wee Irish left-back Billy McCandless — in a squad of 16 players our responsibility was quite apparent.

In that opening game Struth fielded the side that had won the Scottish Cup at Hampden the previous month. We won 8-1, with Jimmy Fleming scoring twice and Jock Buchanan, Andy Cunningham and Alan Morton scoring the others. Our big problems in the early games of the tour were the pitches. Most were bone hard and we were soon complaining of blisters. I don't know how many jars of Vaseline we went through, but we had to use plenty on our feet before every match.

Our next match was in Brooklyn where we beat the local Wanderers 4-0. Andy Cunningham ran the game and Jimmy Fleming scored all four goals. We had 20,000 spectators.

We had been well warned that the toughest match of our tour would be against Fall River in Massachusetts, which was exactly 24 hours after the Brooklyn match. We left Brooklyn on the 11.30 p.m. train, arrived in Massachusetts at 7.30 a.m. and did not feel like playing football. The bunk beds on the train were not in the least comfortable and every time the train went through a station it would let off the most hellish "whoo-oo-ooh" which would have wakened the dead.

I didn't play against Fall River, because the match was on a Sunday.

I never thought the time would come, so early in my career as a Rangers player, that I would have to stand before the awesome Bill

Very much Rangers VIPs of the 1928 tour of America and Canada are: (left to right) Davie Meiklejohn, director Jimmy Bowie, manager Bill Struth, skipper Tommy Muirhead and Andy Cunningham.

Struth, with his strong Victorian principles, and tell him that I could not play for Rangers. It took me a day or two and a number of speech rehearsals before I finally plucked up the courage to say to him: "I'm sorry, but I cannot play football on a Sunday."

Gently, he asked me why. I explained that as my father was a church elder, he had an obvious Christian respect for the Sabbath, and had told me when I left home that while he hoped that I would enjoy the experience of visiting and playing in America and Canada, that I shouldn't play if any of the games were on a Sunday.

Struth looked at me for a moment and then said: "Well, young man, it that's what your father told you and that's the way you feel about it, then I'll leave you out. I understand."

Tommy Muirhead took my place at inside-left — the only change from our Cup-winning side — in what turned out to be one of the toughest matches I've ever seen. Had this been a bit of divine guidance?

43

I wonder! Despite the Christian guidance from my father I never really was one for turning the other cheek, and I know that if I had played in this game I would have been involved right up to the armpits!

Fall River kicked everything above the grass. Three times our 'keeper Tom Hamilton was sent hurtling into the back of the net. How some of the Rangers players didn't suffer broken legs I just don't know. But their skinned knees were something to behold when the game finished without a goal being scored. Billy McCandless, who sat beside me watching the game, thought it was no tougher than a reserve match in Scotland. When Cunningham and Archibald heard what Billy had said they almost exploded. Said Andy: "The match was a bloody disgrace."

Six days later we were guests of Clan Grant in Pittsburgh where Bill Struth was given a gold key to the city. We beat Pittsburg 9-0 and I scored another hat-trick. It was becoming apparent that we were in danger of being smothered by kindness. Every Scottish society of every description wanted us as their guests at lunches, dinners, dances and cocktail parties. As it was, the constant travelling, mostly by overnight train journey, was proving exhausting.

The fourth match of our tour was in Detroit. Another Sunday match. I felt it was decision time for me. How often would I be asked to play for Rangers on a Sunday during my career? I had just finished my first season with the club. Could I continue to say: "Never on a Sunday"?

I talked things over with Struth, who told me he wanted to rest Dougie Gray, Davie Meiklejohn and Sandy Archibald. I played. Willie Hair, our reserve right-winger, scored in a 1-1 draw, with my room-mate Jock Buchanan putting the ball past Tom Hamilton for the Detroit equaliser.

Over 19,000 people turned up for our first match in Canada against a team called Ulster United in Toronto. There were so many Scottish accents here that we could have been playing at Ibrox. I scored four of the goals in a 7-0 win. After this match we lost our two part-timers, Jimmy Fleming and Alan Morton. They had to go back to Scotland to resume their work!

I now had Tommy Muirhead as my left-wing partner and Doc Marshall was at centre-forward. We beat Montreal 5-1 and I got one of the goals. The hospitality and generosity shown to us in Canada was quite overwhelming. When you said farewell to your guests you were struggling to keep a tear out of your eye.

This was the team that beat the Illinois Al-Stars 4-1 in Chicago during the tour of 1928. Players in the back row: (left to right) are Dougie Gray, Jimmy Simpson, Tommy Muirhead, Tom Hamilton, Jock Buchanan, Andy Cunningham and Sandy Archibald. In front: Billy McCandless, Bob McPhail, Jimmy Marshall, Davie Meiklejohn and trainer Jimmy Kerr.

We got a 2-2 draw in Boston, where a former Partick Thistle player called Johnny Ballantyne scored both the Boston goals. We then beat Illinois 4-1 in Chigago where, thank goodness, it rained. Then it was back to the Brooklyn ground for the last match of a most demanding tour, where we beat an American Select 6-0 with the rain again making it easier on the feet.

Well, of course, we had to go to a baseball game, didn't we? And the man we saw was that great American idol "Babe" Ruth playing for the New York Yankees. Here was a man earning 80,000 dollars a year hitting a ball with a bat. This we had to see. He was taller than I expected, 6 ft 2 ins, and he was a left-hander. The American Press, who seem to have a nice turn of phrase, called him "The Sultan of swat", because he had hit a record 714 home runs in 22 major seasons.

I honestly didn't find the game all that exciting. Indeed I found it all rather boring, possibly because I didn't really understand the subtle technicalities of the game. But I do recall getting a chuckle when the gentleman with the big gloves and mesh mask over his face standing behind the flamboyant "Babe" Ruth — I think they call him a catcher — kept sticking a finger up Ruth's backside just before the pitcher threw the ball. Ruth's answer to this bit of backside baiting was to spit at him! It's about the only thing I remember of that particular baseball match.

I also had the pleasure of meeting the great Jack Dempsey but, unfortunately after he had lost his world heavyweight title to Gene Tunney. He had a superb restaurant in New York and we were invited along to dine there as guests. When I shook hands with him I was surprised to find that his hands were extremely soft and fleshy. I was expecting to have my hand crushed to the bone.

The "Manassa Mauler", as they called him, had been world champion for seven years, and was proud that he had been involved in the first five "million-dollar" gate fights. He seemed a very pleasant, friendly man and was obviously very popular. He also served good food.

During one of our matches in the New York area I heard a familiar whistle coming from the stand after I had made a pass. The shock of hearing it made me stop and look towards the crowd. The "whistle" was the rallying call which had been used by my pals and school chums in Barrhead, and they included Tommy McInally, who went on to become an outstanding player with Celtic. When any of us heard this whistle while in our homes, we would nip out into the street, as it usually signalled that someone had some money to buy a bottle of lemonade, a bag of chips or even the full fish supper. It was very much share and share alike with the kids in Barrhead. The mystery of the "whistle" was solved after the match when a boyhood chum of mine named Bob Colquhoun greeted me with a huge smile. Only then was I able to explain to Struth why I had suddenly stopped playing during the match.

There was a really "daft" interlude at a stop we made in Canada, where the engine of our train had to be "watered and fed". Some of us decided to stretch our legs on the platform, others stayed on the train reading or arguing about football. Suddenly over the tannoy system I heard: "Mr Burt McPhail . . . Mr Burt McPhail."

I think I should explain right here that my friends in Barrhead always call me Bert and my close family — even to this day — call me Bertie. I only became known as "Bob" when the Airdrie scout Jock Weir looked at my signature on the Airdrie form said: "Robert? Right, Bob, welcome to the club." "Bob" stuck from that moment . . . but not as far as my friends and family were concerned.

I don't think Jock Weir realised the favour he did me when he changed my name. How could I go on to the football field with a name like Bertie? It made you sound like a pansy. I'm sure you would agree that being referred to as "that dirty big bugger Boab McPhail" has a

We're all looking a bit stiff and formal here, during a visit to the offices of Charles Kline, Mayor of Pittsburgh, prior to our 9-0 win over the local side in 1928.

much more macho sound about it than "that dirty big bugger Bertie McPhail". Agreed?

My Ibrox team-mates were, of course, as intrigued as I was about this tannoy call and were certainly more intrigued when they saw a very attractive young lady striding towards me on the platform. It turned out to be a cousin of mine from Paisley, Helen Baxter, who had emigrated to Canada the year before. Our respective mums were sisters, and very close sisters at that. Before Helen knew what was happening to her, the entire Rangers team lined up on either side of her chanting: "Here comes the bride, here comes the bride." Helen didn't let me down. She grabbed my arm and marched up and down the platform, as the Rangers players *and* Bill Struth had a good laugh along with the other passengers on the train. I was referred to as "Burt" in certain true blue quarters for a long, long time after that.

In all we played ten games in 25 days on that tour before crowds averaging 15,000. We won seven of the games, had three draws and scored 46 goals for the loss of seven. Bill Struth was a very proud and happy man at the end of it all. He felt Rangers had done themselves nothing but good throughout the tour. It had been a success.

Our manager, however, wasn't too happy about the substitutes used by the Americans. In our first match in Philadelphia the Americans had used 14 players. Struth wouldn't countenance Rangers using substitutes. As an old ped, who knew all the dodges of professional running, he felt the Americans had tried to put one over on him. He said: "Subs cannot find a place in our game, not even for an injury. Players could feign injury in order to be replaced. This should not be allowed. Football is a man's game and each team should take its chances of losing a player or two."

How times have changed. Substitutes are now part and parcel of the game throughout the world. And I have no doubts that Struth would have become a master at making the best use out of the extra players on the bench.

We sailed home from New York to Southampton on the SS *Berengaria* and thence by train to Glasgow, where we felt we had earned a rest. It had been a long, hard season, and an arduous tour. But a most momentous one for me, as a first-year Ranger.

We did get one unexpected bonus from the trip — Bob "Whitey" McDonald, who had played against us in Canada. He had impressed Bill Struth with his long throw-ins and good play. When "Whitey" crossed the Atlantic on the Anchor-Donaldson liner the SS *Andania* as a member of the Rangers squad for our second tour of the States and Canada in 1930, he was no longer an unknown. He had won a championship medal and a Scottish Cup medal that season, when he had played right-half against Partick Thistle in the replayed final and, because he had been born in Belfast, he had won his first Irish cap against Scotland at Celtic Park.

We sailed from Greenock to Quebec arriving on a Sunday in May 1930. I remember we became dab hands at deck billiards, quoits and all the other games they played on deck.

We now had an extremely articulate player in our ranks in George Brown, a graduate of Glasgow University, who was a school teacher. He had joined us the previous season and on this trip revealed himself as an accomplished choirmaster. When he learned I could play the piano, he quickly organised entertainment for the passengers. Almost every day we were called upon to give our very special interpretation of *MacNamara's Band.* That was our *pièce de resistance.* I think mainly because we knew the words of that song better than any other.

Because of a head injury I had sustained in the Glasgow Charity Cup final against Celtic, I missed the opening match against Ulster United

Looking extremely natty in our plus-fours, we pause for a farewell picture on the good ship SS California *en route to New York and a 10-match tour of America and Canada, in 1928. This was the Cup-winning squad of that year, namely, (from top to bottom), Tom Hamilton, Dougie Gray, Bob Hamilton, Jock Buchanan, Davie Meiklejohn, Tully Craig, Andy Cunningham, Jimmy Fleming, Bob McPhail, Sandy Archibald and Alan Morton. Also in the picture are directors Jimmy Bowie, trainer Jimmy Kerr, chairman-elect Duncan Graham and manager Bill Struth.*

in Toronto. Tommy Muirhead took my place at inside-left and Brown, later to establish himself as one of the most stylish left-halfs in Scottish football, was at inside-right as stand-in for Doc Marshall, who joined the tour later as a passenger on the *Aquitania*. Alan Morton and Jimmy Fleming scored two goals apiece in a 4-3 win. We then visited Niagara Falls en route to our game in Hamilton against the local Thistle. It was one that "Whitey" McDonald wanted to do well in as his brother was the Thistle's outside-left. Again I was a spectator as the boys won 3-0 with Jimmy Fleming scoring twice and Willie Nicholson getting the other.

We were in no fit condition for our game with the New York Nationals in our third tour game. We had been ten hours on the train prior to the game and not surprisingly found ourselves 3-1 down at half-time. We had young Jimmy Smith, who had played one league game during the season, at centre-forward and Alan Morton and I were together again on the left-wing. Well, we clawed our way back into the game to win 4-3 with Smithie and I scoring two goals apiece.

Another Sunday game, against the notorious, certainly as far as we were concerned, Fall River at New Bedford. I didn't play, simply because I wasn't fit enough. However, the boys won 3-2 with the goals coming from the fast-improving Smith, Davie Meiklejohn and George Brown. A possible bloodbath did not develop.

It surprised none of us that Smith, who was an Airdrie lad, scored a hat-trick in his next match. This was Car Steel in Montreal where we won 5-2 with Brown and I scoring the other goals.

We then travelled to Winnipeg, where we beat Fort Rouge 4-2; then on to Vancouver, where Smith scored another hat-trick in a 5-0 win over Edmonton, and in the same city beat St. Andrews 7-1 where Jimmy Fleming got a hat-trick.

There was never any suggestion that we should ease up in any of our games if we were finding it easy. Bill Struth insisted that we give our best and chase as many goals as we could, as he was determined that his Rangers would provide as much entertainment as possible for the spectators, and leave them with a lasting impression of how we played football.

It was while we were in Canada that we learned that Rangers had made a profit of £6,153-12s-5d during the season just ended, and would be paying their shareholders a ten per cent dividend. The previous season when Kilmarnock had beaten us in the Scottish Cup final and we had won the championship by a massive 16 points from

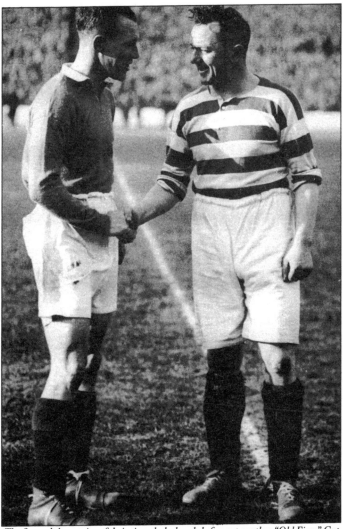

The finest club captains of their time shake hands before yet another "Old Firm" Cup final at Hampden Park. A mid-line meeting between Davie Meiklejohn of Rangers and Willie McStay of Celtic. You can almost see them wetting their lips!

Celtic, the profit had been a modest £1,948-0s-5d. Season tickets for the 1930-31 season would be 30 shillings (or should I say £1.50) and that included tax!

Alan Morton made one of his rare appearances as an outside-right in Victoria, British Columbia, in an 8-1 win over Victoria West. Jimmy Smith hit yet another hat-trick and I scored twice. I sat out our 8-1 win in Calgary against the local United, where Doc Marshall played inside-left and collected his only hat-trick of the tour.

No rest for the weary. We were back in America again where we beat Sparta 4-1 in Chicago on a very acceptable wet day, beat a Detroit Select in that city under floodlights 3-1, and then defeated Bruels in Cleveland, Ohio, 3-1, again under floodlights.

We finished our tour on 22 June in New York, beating Fall River 6-1. Jimmy Smith scored four times to bring his total to 18 goals, four better than Jimmy Fleming and 11 better than me! Struth now knew he had an extremely talented young centre-forward ready, and very able, to take over from Jimmy Fleming in the season ahead, though "Flem" had no intention of standing aside. It produced healthy competition for a vital place in the Rangers team over the next two or three seasons.

As a public relations exercise for Rangers the tour had been a wonderful success. We had played 14 games and won them all. We had scored 68 goals and lost 20. "Will ye' no' come back again" are the words of the song Bill Struth had to deal with before we left every city we had visited.

Oh . . . we came back with another wee "bonus". This time his name was Bob McAulay who, it was discovered, had been born in Wishaw. He had been at left-back for Fall River in that rough and tumble match in 1928 when we were held to a goalless draw, and he was still there in both matches of the 1930 tour. Struth noted how well he had played against Sandy Archibald and Jimmy Fleming, our right-wingers in the matches with Fall River, and decided to sign him. McAulay, who became Rangers' chief scout in the Edinburgh area when his playing days were over, soon became a permanent member of the Rangers team, and indeed gained two Scotland caps against Northern Ireland and Wales in 1932.

Bill Struth could pick 'em!

5

The Tragedy of Thomson's Last Save

I knew John Thomson had been seriously injured when I ran over to him as he lay, barely conscious, on the turf of Ibrox on that tragic day of 5 September, 1931. His face was out of alignment. It was an accident, let there be no doubts about that. It happened just five minutes after the second half of an "Old Firm" match that had given the huge crowd little entertainment. There had been no goals in the first half, but suddenly it looked as though Sam English would put us into the lead. Our skipper David Meiklejohn had sent Jimmy Fleming, who was at outside-right that day, scampering down the wing. Jimmy managed to slip past the uncompromising "Peter" McGonagle before sending the ball into the Celtic penalty area, just ahead of English.

Thomson, a real artist of a 'keeper, immediately came off his line, hesitated fractionally on the six-yards line to balance himself, and then threw himself at the ball which was now at Sam's feet. I was just two yards away.

John's head struck Sam's left knee and both players went down. Sam told me later that he hadn't felt any pain in his knee, but for several days after the incident you could see clearly tooth marks on the fleshy part close to his knee cap.

There were jeers from the Rangers fans behind the Celtic goal as Thomson lay on the ground with players anxiously circling round him. I remember Meiklejohn standing up, looking at the Rangers fans and indicating to them to be quiet, by waving his hands up and down. There was a sudden eerie silence. Fleming and Jimmy McStay began to wave for a stretcher, as the worst memory of my career began to unfold.

John Thomson died at 9.25 that night in Glasgow's Victoria Infirmary. His injury had been a depressed fracture of the skull. I learned of his death as I walked from Davie Rombach's restaurant in

Hope Street, after a meal, towards the *Sunday Mail* office nearby, where I had hoped to get some information on the Celtic goalkeeper.

I cried. I just couldn't stop myself. The tears just flowed down my cheeks, as I stood in the street uncertain what to do with myself. I just couldn't believe that one of football's gentlemen, one of the nicest lads I had ever met in the game, was dead.

Poor Sam English was devastated. He never, ever recovered. It was a tragedy that was to haunt him for the rest of his life, all the way to his death in Vale of Leven hospital in 1967. Sam was in the right place at the wrong time. It could have been me. It could have been Jimmy Fleming. It could have been Doc Marshall. The Old Firm players learned about fate that day.

After the game, which finished without any goals, Bill Struth had told Sam to get home as quickly as possible and not to worry about things. "We'll take care of everything," he said. Davie Meiklejohn tried to cheer him up with a smile, shouting: "You'll be all right, Blondie." I think it was Tom Hamilton who drove him home to Dalmuir.

There was, of course, a fatal accident inquiry which completely exonerated English. But to this day I can never understand the statement of the Celtic manager, Willie Maley. He said: "I saw a clash when the men came together. Both fell, but Thomson could not rise. I hope it was an accident, but I did not see enough to enable me to form an opinion."

Now why did Maley say that? There was never the slightest doubt in the minds of every player on the field at Ibrox that day that it *had* been an accident. It was a shocking statement to make in front of a court of inquiry. I never forgave the man for what he said. You can imagine the effect it had on English, and his family. He had just joined Rangers two months before, was a mere 21 years of age, and the tragedy happened in his first ever game against Celtic.

Years later Sam described himself as "the second-unluckiest footballer in the world". Often he would ask himself: "Why did it have to be me?"

The entire Rangers playing staff attended the funeral of John Thomson near his home in Cardenden, Fife. There must have been 30,000 people there, with thousands buying the special four shillings excursion train ticket from Glasgow to Fife. Many unemployed people actually walked from Glasgow. There were two memorial services in Glasgow, and I recall Davie Meiklejohn, our captain, reading the lesson at one of them.

Celtic manager Willie Maley and Jimmy McStay help to carry the coffin bearing the body of John Thomson. One of football's saddest moments.

The circumstances of his death established John Thomson as a legend. If he had lived I'm convinced he would still have established himself as one of the game's unforgettable personalities. He was just 22 years old.

I got to know him quite well. Apart from playing against him as a Rangers player, I played with him in the Scotland team and the Scottish League side, where his international reputation was assured. On sheer merit he had replaced Jack Harkness, of the "wizards" fame, as Scotland's No. 1 and had indeed lost just one goal in his four games for Scotland prior to his death.

Now there was a bit of a clique when the Scottish players met prior to an international — the Celtic and Rangers players invariably sat together. This may surprise the modern-day supporters who dedicate their lives to the terracings of Ibrox and Celtic Park, but because we had so much in common, and were players who were expected to win every game in which we played, we would sit together and talk about football. We had a great respect for each other. It was then I really got to know Thomson. He was a quiet lad who had been a miner in his native Fife and would talk about the games he had played in, his ambitions, how he enjoyed playing for Scotland so much and would discuss various players. I liked him. He was a very popular young man, with a great future in football.

Chic Geatons, the left-half, took over from Thomson in goal when he was carried from the ground on a stretcher. But the game had lost any real meaning as most of us were worrying about what had happened to the young Celtic 'keeper. Later Chic said: "The sympathy of every Celtic player is with Sam English. If there is one player who would have avoided that impact, if he could, it would have been English. He is not a rough player."

Sam had never spoken to John Thomson in his life. Just before the interval Sam went up for a high ball from the right, but Thomson quite calmly plucked the ball away from his head. "Hard lines, young fellow," said Thomson. These were the only words English ever heard Thomson speak.

Though Thomson had deflected the ball from English away from his goal for a corner-kick when he made that fatal save, when play resumed the referee, Willie Holborn, gave a goal-kick. Quite significantly there was no foul given.

Our manager, Bill Struth, refused to let Sam hide away with his young wife and daughter. Two days after Thomson's funeral, Sam played against Third Lanark in the first round of the Glasgow Charity Cup at Ibrox. He didn't want to play — that was clear to all of us. But Struth told him: "Keep your eye on the ball and remember to play football." It was the right decision. We won 4-1 and I think Sam scored. But did it really matter?

His father had advised him to start a new life in America. Though Sam lived in Clydebank, he had been born in Coleraine in Northern Ireland, where his father had lived. His father wanted him to get out of the country, because he was convinced his son would never be allowed to forget it. He was right.

The remarkable scenes following the funeral of Celtic 'keeper John Thomson at Bowhill Cemetery in Fife, when an estimated 30,000 people filed past the memorial stone at his grave. His sudden and tragic death affected every working-class family in Scotland, such was his popularity.

In our first match at Parkhead after the tragedy there were shouts of "murderer" and "watch the killer" any time Sam went near the ball. He was scared to go anywhere near a 'keeper. It was all so cruel. Struth even suggested he should put cotton wool in his ears to block out the shouts. I really felt very sorry for the young fellow. He would sit next to me before every game as we got stripped to play. You found you ran out of things to say.

But this superb footballer had a lot of guts. He stuck it out. And astonishingly in this, his first season with Rangers, he smashed every scoring record at Ibrox! Sam scored 44 goals in 35 league games, an average of 1.25 a game, and scored nine in the various cup-ties. A total of 53 goals in his first season as a senior. A season in which he had been persecuted, vilified and indeed immortalised for all the wrong reasons. *It was 32 years before that record was broken at Ibrox.* The new record was established by Jim Forrest, who scored 30 goals in 30 league games and scored another 26 goals in 20 cup-ties, including six in the European Cup. Sam's 44 league goals is still a record.

I've been asked many times by many people over the last half century: Who was the best centre-forward you every played with? It was Sam English. Even before he joined Rangers he had proved his ability to be a scorer. As a Junior with Yoker Athletic he had scored 293 goals in three seasons!

Yes, Sam was better than Hughie Gallacher. Yes, he was better than Jimmy McGrory. Yes, he was better than Jimmy Fleming. Yes, he was better than Jimmy Smith. Though I never played with the great Dixie Dean of Everton, I did play against him. I would have taken English before him. They were all different types of players, of course, and they all had many qualities.

I couldn't fault English. He was lightning. He was fast on his feet and fast in thought. He was unselfish. If he thought you were in a better position than he was then he would give you the ball to score. He seemed to dart away from centre-halfs. Though he was just five feet seven and a half inches in height, he was good with his head. Sam was so quick-thinking that when he gave you the ball he gave you time to think what you should do with it. Return the pass, hold it and find your left-winger or hit a long one to the right? He laid on many of my goals in that unforgettable season. It was a pleasure to play with him, and I'm sure if he hadn't been haunted by the horror of the John Thomson tragedy he would have become one of the finest centre-forwards ever at Ibrox.

I was glad that he was a member of our cup-winning side that season against Kilmarnock. He deserved to be a winner . . . just once. The strain of the publicity was always present however and no matter where English would go people would point at him. He had become a curiosity, a moving peepshow. Only time would be the healer, but footballers don't have too much time. And time was already running out for Sam.

It was obvious that something had died within him. The close season had given him no respite. He scored just 10 goals in his 25 league games the following season, but he did help me to score 30 goals in the 31 league games I played and was a help in aiding big Jimmy Smith to settle into the side as a regular team member. Smithie scored 33 goals in 34 league appearances.

It surprised no one when English was transferred to Liverpool at the end of the season. He had had enough. But the Thomson tragedy followed him to England, where opponents would taunt him with what had happened at Ibrox. He drifted back to Scotland to Queen of the South, then on to Hartlepool United. At the age of 28 he quit.

Many years later he wrote an article in the *Scottish Daily Express*. He described his career as seven years of joyless sport. A sad epithet.

The only time Celtic 'keeper John Thomson and Rangers centre-forward Sam English played against each other. The fateful match of 1931 at Ibrox, where Thomson lost his life saving from English. John punches clear as Sam turns away.

The "Old Firm" teams on that unforgettable September day of 1931 were: *Rangers*: Dawson; Gray and McAulay; Meiklejohn, Simpson, Brown; Fleming, Marshall, English, McPhail and Morton. *Celtic*: Thomson; Cook, McGonagle; Wilson, J. McStay, Geatons; R. Thomson, A. Thomson, McGrory, Scarff, Napier. The crowd was 80,000. The score was 0-0. No one had been a winner that day.

In naming Sam English as the centre-forward I preferred to play with in a marvellous era of great scorers, is not to detract from the other household names of that time.

Hughie Gallacher, whose life became a self-inflicted tragedy, was a scoring genius, with 387 goals in 543 league games on either side of the border. But he was a selfish player. He really didn't play for the team. Wee Hughie wanted to score all the goals. He was a glory seeker who sought adulation and publicity. You had to respect his abilities, because he was so good at tucking the ball into the net, but as I've said elsewhere in this book I did not like him as a person. He was the kind of man who would have started a fight in an empty house.

Jimmy McGrory on the other hand was a marvellous team man. He would play his heart out for his team and his team-mates. Jimmy rarely complained about a bad pass and would chase the ball all over the place. He had courage and he had great strength. To score 397 goals in 378 league games for Celtic was quite remarkable. I played against him dozens of times and with him in a Scottish jersey. I had nothing but admiration for the man. He was simply unlucky to be around when Gallacher was at his peak as a Scotland player, Jimmy's heading power was legend and though he is mainly remembered for scoring eight goals in a league match against Dunfermline, I recall him scoring four goals in five minutes against Motherwell. He was a machine.

Jimmy Fleming, who joined the club from St. Johnstone in 1925, played in three Rangers cup-winning sides alongside me. He was a hard-working centre-forward who just happened to be playing in one of the best Rangers teams of all time. Like Alan Morton, he was a part-timer, so I only saw him on match days. He was good at finishing off the work of others, and in nine seasons at Ibrox he scored 170 league goals in 219 games, and 57 cup goals in 70 ties. He gave good value for money.

Jimmy Smith had more to offer as a striker. He was big, nimble on his feet, had superb timing in the air, and would kid the life out of opponents with his patter. Jimmy scored some really smart goals in his time. In ten seasons with the club, up until the war years, he scored 224

Celtic 'keeper John Thomson comfortably deals with a Rangers attack during a Glasgow Charity Cup tie, while his full-back Willie "Peter" McGonagle seems intent in doing big Jimmy Smith no good at all.

league goals and 45 cup goals. He was a clever footballer.

The great English centre-forward of that time was Dixie Dean of Everton, but because of injury problems he played only 16 times for his country. Like Gallacher and McGrory he was a prolific scorer. Like McGrory he was strong, had powerful shoulders and was quite brilliant in the air. He scored 347 goals for his beloved Everton in league football, which is a record. This included an astonishing burst of 60 goals in one season. England claim him as the best centre-forward in history. He was good, but to me "wee Hughie" and McGrory were better.

Sam? Well we never really got to know how great he would have become. I only know he was the centre-forward I enjoyed playing alongside more than any other.

6

Why I Never Ever Played at Wembley

It has to be the burning ambition of any Scot worth his boots to play for his country at Wembley. To meet and to beat England on their own backyard is something that every player hopes can be part of his career.

I was playing with Airdrie when the inaugural Wembley match between the two countries was played in 1924, when the crowd was a mere 37,250. It wasn't a game to remember, finishing 1-1 with the English 'keeper Eric Taylor of Huddersfield being rather unkindly given the credit for scoring Scotland's goal. What actually happened was that a shot from the Scottish right-half, Willie Clunas of Sunderland, hit a post, rebounded on to Taylor's body and finished in the net. I'd have given the goal to Clunas!

It took the 1928 match to make the blood pump with frightening passion through the veins of Scots all over the world. The day the "wizards" crushed England 5-1 before a rain-soaked crowd of 80,868 and established this piece of English soil as a mecca for generations of Scots with hair on their chests and football as their religion.

The displays of patriotism by Scots at Wembley since then have been outrageous, frenzied and gallus. It has become a lost weekend for Scots from every neuk and cranny stretching from Lockerbie to Lochboisdale. A biennial pilgrimage for thousands which does nothing for their health, or their pockets . . . but does no harm to the whisky trade. Just to experience "Wemba-lee" is enough for some. Others in borrowed kilts — "Oh to see oorselves as 'ithers see us!" — tartan bunnet, and little else, have travelled south seeking a re-run of that legendary "wizards" win . . . sadly in vain.

The millions of Scots who have gone to Wembley for this England-Scotland confrontation from these early days will therefore find it a bit difficult to understand why I refused to play at Wembley.

Not only have I never played there, I've never seen the place.

My love of Rangers proved to be greater than the chance to play in this famous game, which brings out the best and the worst in Scottish supporters. I found myself in a rather unique tug-of-war. The chance was there for me to play for Scotland at Wembley, at least twice, but I said "No" for reasons which seemed important to me at the time. My priority was simply Rangers Football Club, and I found that the more I played in the light blue jersey, the more dedicated I became to the club. Of course I'm disappointed that I never played at Wembley. Regretful? I don't think so. I made my choice and all these years later I still think I did the right thing. It was the very success of Rangers which really prevented me from playing in the famous London ground. Let me explain.

While I was at Ibrox, the Wembley matches with England were played during the even years, and I suppose I was most eligible for the Scottish team in the years of 1928, 1930, 1932, 1934 and 1936. Now it just so happens that Rangers were in the final of the Scottish Cup — to be played one week after the Wembley match — in each of these particular years!

I have to say right away that while I was considered for a place in the unforgettable match of '28, I wasn't chosen. The selectors decided that they preferred two wee fellows at inside-forward in Jimmy Dunn of Hibs and Alex James of Preston North End, baggy breeks and all, to the two big greetin'-faced Rangers inside-forwards, Andy Cunningham and Bob McPhail, who had played against England at Hampden the previous year when we lost 2-1. I was at that time, however, an Airdrie player. There can be no argument with their choice after a 5-1 win. And you know, maybe part of the "wizards" mystique was that Alan Morton was the only Rangers player in the side, and Celtic didn't have anyone.

I was under no illusions that I was an automatic choice for Scotland at any time of my career. There were too many outstanding inside-forwards about for me to get carried away. Players like Jimmy Dunn, Bobby Rankin of St. Mirren, George Stevenson of Motherwell, Charlie Napier of Celtic, Jim Easson of Portsmouth, Willie Mills of Aberdeen, Andy Black of Hearts and many, many more.

I had a niggling injury prior to the 1930 game, and I suggested to manager Bill Struth that it might be a good idea if I avoided Wembley, even if chosen as a reserve, to make sure I was fit for the cup final with Partick Thistle. Struth didn't need any convincing. The Wembley inside-forwards then were James and Stevenson. The Scots lost 5-2 and there were five Rangers in the side, namely Jock Buchanan, Dougie Gray, Tully Craig, Jimmy Fleming and Davie Meiklejohn. They were not in a good humour when I suggested in the Ibrox dressing-room that they had lacked the help I normally gave them every Saturday.

Now, at this time, Rangers had just won the League Championship for a fifth successive season and were determined to regain the Scottish Cup which they had lost to Kilmarnock the previous season. All kinds of records were beckoning and we were convinced we had the players to break them, with considerable encouragement from Bill Struth. At that time Meiklejohn was the club captain and I was the vice-captain. Struth made sure that "Meek" kept everybody on their toes at the back and that with my natural ability to moan at people, I should keep the forwards in order. It goes without saying that I was fit enough to play in the 1930 final which we won, after a replay.

Two years later and there were again "doubts" too about Meiklejohn. "Mr" Struth helped us make up our minds. He told "Meek" and myself: "I feel you'd be better with a week's rest before our final with Kilmarnock. But make up your own minds. Go and have a fitness test and see how you feel." Well "Meek" and I went through the charade of running up and down the field, and as a nod is as good as a wink, we pulled out of Wembley. We were both of course fit to play in the final, which we won 3-0 after a replay. Again Rangers had five players in that Wembley team and again Scotland lost by three goals, 3-0. Tom Hamilton, George Brown, Sandy Archibald, Doc Marshall and Alan Morton all played. "Meek" and I said nothing!

It sounded very like another outbreak of Meiklejohn and McPhail Wembley withdrawal symptoms in 1934. I have to say though that I was quite badly injured when I captained the Scottish League team against the English League at Ibrox in February when I managed to score in a 2-2 draw. It was one of those injuries which didn't really clear up until the close season. Meiklejohn was also struggling with an injury. So much so that not only was he not fit enough to be considered for the Wembley team of that year, he wasn't fit enough to play in the final against St. Mirren, when Jimmy Kennedy replaced him at right-half. After a talk with Bill Struth it was decided that I wouldn't be available for Wembley. But of course I did play in the final which Rangers won 5-0.

Now, during that Wembley weekend, my wife, Jessie, and I decided

It must have been a good day in Glasgow, as I get the deck chair out and settle down for a bit of reading in my back garden.

to go down to Dumfries to visit a good friend of mine, Willie Stewart, who had played alongside me in my Junior days with Pollok. We stayed the weekend. Willie's home was very close to the main railway line from Glasgow to London, but was a little bit out from the station at Dumfries. When a train pulled up just outside his window on the Sunday I looked out to see what was going on. It was packed with Scots fans returning from Wembley, who were suffering from too much drink, too little sleep and another 3-0 defeat by England. They were not in a good humour.

Several of them recognised me and began shouting my name. They were looking for a scapegoat and they had just found one. Me! They called me everything but my christian name. I've never closed a window as quickly in my life. They seemed to think that I was some sort of traitor. The only Rangers player who had played in that Wembley game was Doc Marshall, our inside-right.

There was very little chance of me playing in the 1936 Wembley match as I had played just 26 out of the 38 league fixtures that season because of a variety of injuries. And I wanted to make sure I would play in the final against Third Lanark. So my last real chance of playing at Wembley had gone, though a Rangers player did play at inside-left: Alex Venters. Alex, though he preferred playing on the left side of the field, had established himself as our inside-right, and had scored 17 goals in 32 league games. The Wembley inside-right was Tommy Walker of Hearts, who scored from the penalty-spot, to give the Scots a 1-1 draw.

In what proved to be my last Scottish Cup final I scored the only goal against Third Lanark.

The fee for playing for Scotland in these days was £6 and of course you kept your jersey, and got a cap at the end of each season. Bill Struth made sure I suffered no financial loss any time I had to pull out of an international squad. When I did, my wages at Ibrox the following week would contain an extra £6! Struth never ever scrimped as far as Rangers was concerned. He demanded the best, and was always prepared to pay for it.

Looking back now at those glorious years of Ibrox supremacy of which I was proud to be part, I must have been making, for the most part, a club or country decision almost subconsciously in these eventful even years from 1928 to 1936. Did I make the right decisions? Well, in each of these "even" years I not only played in a Scottish Cup final, I played in a winning Rangers team. Five wins out of five starts. The sixth medal I won with Rangers was in 1935 when we beat Hamilton Accies 2-1. Would I have played in so many finals for Rangers if I had made the trip to London, always by train in these days, and risked injury or, in some circumstances, aggravation of a niggly strain? I don't think so.

In a way Struth was paying me a tremendous compliment in making it abundantly clear he wanted me fit and well in his cup final team because he must have felt my experience and influence was vital, even though he released other players for the Wembley match. Now, never at any time did he tell me not to play at Wembley. The decision was always left to myself but the man knew me better than I knew myself. He knew that if I played at Wembley I'd give it 100 per cent because I tried to give this game I loved everything I had every time out. I was only interested in being a winner. So when Struth suggested I'd be none the

Venters shoots for goal against Clyde, with me as an interested spectator.

worse of a week's rest before a final, he was suggesting he wanted a McPhail who was as fit as possible, at that particular time of the season.

I think it was this competitive spirit in my make-up that stopped me becoming a permanent captain at Ibrox. On the occasions I was skipper, usually when "Meek" was out with an injury, I instinctively tried to do the job of others and perhaps spent too much time back helping out in defence. I think I took my responsibility as team captain too much to heart, and fortunately Struth saw it. He wanted me greetin' at the rest of the forwards, and getting things moving up front.

It had to be sheer coincidence that I always seemed to be fit and available to play against England at Hampden. Or maybe it was the fact that on three of the occasions I didn't have a Scottish Cup final week later! As a Rangers player — and remember I had been capped against England earlier as an Airdrie man — I played against England in 1931, 1933, 1935 and 1937 and finished on the winning side on each occasion.

In the first of these games our skipper, Davie Meiklejohn, was quite brilliant in everything he did, hardly giving the great Everton centre-forward "Dixie" Dean a sniff at the ball. Scotland won 2-0 and I felt that my other Ibrox team-mates, wingers Sandy Archibald and Alan Morton, had contributed most to our win through the way they kept tantalising and turning the English defenders. It was Sandy who laid the foundation of Scotland's first goal that day with a powerful corner kick which hit the English left-back Ernie Blenkinsop, and caused their 'keeper Harry Hibbs to fumble it. George Stevenson was quick to get his foot to it and volley the ball into the net. Two minutes later a bit of Alan Morton magic laid on the second goal for Jimmy McGrory. We had all worked hard in a win we fully deserved.

The 1933 match produced a quite volcanic controversial aside which was to finish the international career of one of the most influential players in the British game. Five days before the match, Alex James, now under the influence of the flamboyant Herbert Chapman of Arsenal, pulled out because he was unfit. As I remember, I had been named as the inside-right with James at inside-left. I felt a bit peeved at this, as I had never played anywhere else but inside-left with a Scottish side or indeed with Rangers. Why should James get my place? However, with wee Alex pulling out I moved to the left side of the field and my Ibrox team-mate Doc Marshall came in at inside-right.

Well, we beat England 2-1 with the quite mercurial Jimmy McGrory scoring both goals. I must say I had the utmost pleasure laying on the winner for Jimmy eight minutes from the end. It was one of those moves that you carry with you through your career. I managed to survive a tackle, before pushing the ball through to McGrory. The Celtic forward let fly with a tremendous left-foot shot which hit the roof of the net, leaving Harry Hibbs grabbing at fresh air.

If I knew nothing about the "Hampden Roar" before that moment, I certainly felt the full force of it right there and then. The noise from the crowd of 134,710 which was then a record, must have broken every window within a mile's radius. If it frightened the life out of the English players, I can assure you it damned well scared me. It was a waste of time shouting at each other in the closing minutes, because none of us on that field could hear a thing. We simply floated towards the final whistle on a vast tidal wave of noise.

We had a surprise visit from the great Sir Harry Lauder before this match. I couldn't believe how small he was when he "wachled" into our dressing-room, generally wished us all the best of luck, then got his eyes on our right-winger Jimmy Crawford, the speed merchant from Queen's Park. "Forget the crowd, son," he said to Jimmy. "Play the same wie as ye'd play oan any Setterday." A wee bit taken aback by Sir Harry's personal advice, Jimmy just nodded in silence. As soon as the great man had departed he turned to me and said: "What do you think, Bob?" I said: "Just you get down that wing as fast as you can, and get the ball over even quicker."

Jimmy was no Sandy Archibald, but as befits a Scottish sprint champion, I knew his remarkable pace would have Blenkinsop, his direct opponent, huffing and puffing ... which it did. Meiklejohn missed this one because of injury. His replacement at centre-half was a surprise, Bob Gillespie of Queen's Park, who was coming near the end of his playing life. And he was made captain. Nice way to end his international career.

Some time after the game I learned that Alex James had turned out for Arsenal against Aston Villa. A miracle recovery? I can't recall whether Arsenal won that game, but I do know they won the championship that season with "baggy breeks" as captain. Alex, a cartoonist's delight because of his knee-length pants, was never again to play for Scotland. The selectors turned their backs on him. There was little doubt in my mind that Chapman had "influenced" him to miss the Hampden game and play for Arsenal instead. But, with my Wembley background, who was I to criticise James for not turning up at Hampden?

Though James was very much the architect of the Arsenal success story at that time, he was very much the scorer in his early days with Raith Rovers and Preston, and of course scored twice against England in the "wizards" match of 1928. Chapman, however, saw in the skilful footwork of Alex the player he needed to organise his attacking play and bought him for £9,000 from Preston North End in 1929.

Alex, who was never one to suffer fools gladly and was only too ready

69

to voice his opinion on the rights and wrongs of the game, became a master at turning the defence into attack with his long-range passing from the back, mainly to his left-wing partner Cliff Bastin. He won four championship medals with Arsenal and two F.A. Cup medals. But remarkably in 231 league games for them scored just 26 goals. I don't think I've known a player to change the personality of his play so dramatically as Alex James.

I thought Scotland's full-backs Andy Anderson of Hearts and George Cummings of Partick Thistle were outstanding in the 1935 win over England. My left-wing partner Dally Duncan of Derby County claimed the match as his because he scored the only two goals, which were both headers from Charlie Napier corner kicks. I wasn't all that pleased with my own form, as I missed what I considered two very good chances in the first half. But I thought I compensated for my lost goal touch with a lot of sheer hard work in the second half.

Our skipper that day was big Jimmy Simpson, another Ibrox team-mate. When I think back to Jimmy coming into the Rangers side and the Scotland side it was the beginning of a change in the tactics of the game. Jimmy, a tall man, was very much the stopper centre-half. The man he replaced, Davie Meiklejohn, was a born footballer with brilliant passing skills. It was easy for "Meek" to move to right-half to accommodate Simpson in the side. But it gave Rangers a very strong back four. Two centre-backs, one pushing the ball about and creating attacking moves, the other anchored in defence, using his height of 6 feet to best advantage. Come to think of it, is there anything really new in this great game of football?

My last game against England was on a very special occasion — 17 April, 1937 — when a world record crowd of 149,415 paid to watch, with another 10,000 packed into the ground through totally illegal means of entry. Scotland gave value for money on this occasion, winning 3-1 and I was denied the opportunity of my only international hat-trick by England's new 'keeper, Vic Woodley of Chelsea, just after the restart of the game. I hit the ball right on the button at the right time and I was convinced I had scored until Woodley produced a really great save. No wonder he went on to win another 18 caps for England!

There are those who say this was my finest game for Scotland. All I can say is that I enjoyed it immensely. We found ourselves a goal down just before the interval when the Stoke City centre-forward Freddie Steele beat Jerry Dawson with a really good shot. Two minutes after the interval Scotland's new centre-forward, Frank O'Donnell from

Preston North End, got the equaliser. Thereafter the "Hampden Roar" terrified the English. Some time later the new England outside-right, a laddie called Stanley Matthews, told journalists: "If ever a match was won and lost by a roar, it was this one." Maybe so, but I think I helped a wee bit because I scored two goals in the closing ten minutes.

In the 80th minute I got a good through pass from O'Donnell, who had played very well in his first international, and ran on to belt the ball into the net from about 15 yards. Then in the last minute Jimmy Delaney of Celtic sent a header into the box and I was there to head it into the net. It was one of those games where Scotland got the passes going and I found myself working well with young Tommy Walker of Hearts and my Ibrox team-mate George Brown at my back.

Now Walker had an unusual international career. He made his debut in 1934 against Wales and held his position at inside-right for a further 19 successive internationals until the outbreak of World War II. Tommy was a beautifully balanced player with a lot of style, but he was such a refined, quiet person off the field that it wasn't surprising to see him shy away a little from the heavy physical stuff when the going got a bit rough, particularly at club level.

I went out of my way to make him at ease on these internationals, because I instinctively liked him and enjoyed playing with him. He was a good listener and a quick learner. He was a gentleman in a man's world, even when he became a most successful manager with Hearts after the war.

Years after that 1937 match I was standing on the terracing at another Hampden occasion with a group of friends when a chap nearby started telling us how he'd nearly been crushed to death watching this win over England. He told us: "You just couldn't move. If you put your hands in your pockets you couldn't get them out again, and if you managed to get your hands in the air to cheer the boys on, you couldn't get them down again." I said to him: "That's funny. There was plenty of space where I was." He said: "You must be kidding. The ground was packed tight." "Not where I was," I said. A bit angry now he said: "And where were you?" I then pointed on to the field and told him with a smile: "I was out there!" The look on that man's face was something to behold.

My international career ended rather abruptly when I was 32 years of age. The last of my 17 games for Scotland was on 10 November, 1937 against Northern Ireland at Pittodrie, the ground of Aberdeen. It didn't go well for me. I got a bad injury in the second half when I collided with the Manchester United 'keeper Tom Breen and had to be carried off on a stretcher. However, I managed to stagger back on to the field after 15 minutes and limped out the rest of the game on the left-wing where I wasn't much good to anyone.

Peter Doherty, then with Manchester City, was at his best in this game and scored for the Irishmen in the first half. Jimmy Smith took a pass from Tommy Walker three minutes after the interval for the equaliser in a 1-1 draw. It was a fair result.

In all I played five times against Northern Ireland and managed to get myself on the score sheet three times. There was little to be said about my first appearance in February 1931 in Belfast. It finished a goalless draw with our 'keeper John Thomson failing to get a touch of the ball during the opening 40 minutes. A gale-force wind completely spoiled the game. An all-tartan side had to be fielded in this game because the Football League refused to allow their clubs to release players for internationals to any other country, other than England. It followed a furious row over some English clubs releasing their players and others forcing them to play with their clubs. Our home-based side in that goal-less match was: Thomson (Celtic); Crapnell (Airdrie), Nibloe (Kilmarnock); Wilson (Celtic), Walker (St. Mirren), Hill (Aberdeen); Murdoch (Motherwell), Scarff (Celtic), Yorston (Aberdeen), McPhail (Rangers), Morton (Rangers).

The experience didn't do much for Johnny Murdoch, Peter Scarff and Benny Yorston. They never played for Scotland again. This was the one and only occasion they ever got a cap. These things can happen to you when you take part in a bad game.

Just seven months later we met the Irishmen again, this time at Ibrox. Though Davie Meiklejohn missed a penalty kick, we won 3-1. Our scorers were George Stevenson, Jimmy McGrory and yours truly. The following year in Belfast I got two of the goals in a convincing 4-0 win. Our other scorers were Jimmy McGrory and a new cap, Jamie King from Hamilton Accies, who was my left-wing partner.

Though I scored in the 1933 match at Celtic Park, it wasn't enough and we lost 2-1. My goal came after an hour from a smart ball from Alex Massie of Hearts. But my recollection is that this game belonged to the Irish 'keeper, the great Elisha Scott of Liverpool, who was to play 30 times for his country over a 16-year period. He had a real daft day. It included saving a penalty kick from "Peter" McGonagle of Celtic, who was our skipper. My direct opponent thoroughly enjoyed the result, as he happened to be the Rangers reserve inside-right Alex Stevenson! It was another four years before I faced the Irishmen again, the game which proved to be my last in a Scotland strip.

I never did manage to score against Wales in my three games against them. My first appearance against them was in October 1928 at Ibrox, just seven months after the famous victory of the "wizards" at Wembley. I was the only change from the Wembley attack, replacing Alex James at inside-left. That "wizards" team was to prove an historic one-off. They never did play together again. Against Wales there was no Nelson, Law, Gibson, Bradshaw or James. They were replaced by Dougie Gray, Danny Blair, Tommy Muirhead, Queen's Park centre-half Willie King, and of course myself.

My old Airdrie team-mate, Hughie Gallacher, soon sorted out the men of Wales with a hat-trick so typical of him in the first half. That other "wizard" Jimmy Dunn got the fourth goal in a highly entertaining 4-2 win watched by a crowd of 55,000.

Bertie Thomson of Celtic scored in his only Scotland appearance in my second game against Wales in Wrexham in 1931, where we had to come from behind to win 3-1. Jimmy McGrory and George Stevenson were our other scorers.

My final game against Wales in 1937 in Cardiff proved to be one of the most frustrating of my career. The Welshmen used the offside trap throughout the game and we lost 2-1. To be fair to Bryn Jones and his mates, they had to play the final 20 minutes with just 10 men with their backs to the wall. Alex Massie got Scotland's crumb of comfort.

I played four times against foreign opposition without loss. The match in Paris in 1932 against France was a bit of a landmark as far as Scottish international football was concerned. It was Alan Morton's last appearance in a dark blue strip and the only occasion in which he played against a foreign side as a Scotland player. It was his 31st cap. He had already established a British record of 30 caps in the home international series stretching from 1920, when he was with Queen's Park, to the match with England the previous month.

Alan finished in a winning side. We beat France 3-0 with Neilly Dewar of Third Lanark scoring a hat-trick in the opening 35 minutes. Neilly got a fair bit of help from Alan and I in getting his hat-trick. The *Daily Record* newspaper in Glasgow decided to employ Hughie Gallacher, then with Chelsea, to write their report of the match. I almost blushed when I read what the wee man wrote about me. "Bob McPhail showed again why he is one of the best inside-forwards in football." Well at least he was honest!

73

We got tougher opposition from Austria at Hampden the following season when we drew 2-2. The Austrians certainly didn't like it when their 'keeper Peter Platzer was flattened by a shoulder charge from Motherwell's Willie McFadyen early in the game. Things got a bit rough thereafter. But as I was never one to shirk a bit of physical conflict, I thoroughly enjoyed myself. Indeed I thought Dally Duncan and I had a pretty good day of it on the left wing, and though we twice went into the lead we eventually had to settle for the draw. Davie Meiklejohn got our first goal with a superb free kick and McFadyen got the second when he latched on to a header of mine, which came off the crossbar, and stuck it away.

The previous season Willie had established an all-time Scottish league record by scoring 52 goals for Motherwell in 34 league games — beating Jimmy McGrory's record by three goals. No wonder Motherwell pipped Rangers for the championship that season!

Adolf Hitler's Germany taught us a lot about defensive discipline when we met them at Hampden in 1936, the year of the Jesse Owens Olympics in Berlin. I recall the game being delayed for some 20 minutes because the Germans had got themselves lost in a traffic jam on their way to the Queen's Park ground.

It took the irrepressible enthusiasm of Jimmy Delaney to break down the German defence when he picked up a rebound to score, and then hit a real beauty of a second goal just ten minutes from time, injuring himself in the process. Jimmy was carted off. But back he came with just a few minutes to go and almost got his hat-trick. It was a very satisfying 2-0 win.

I had no great liking for the Germans at that time. Three years earlier I had been on tour with Rangers when we played five games in Germany and one in Vienna. I remember being roughly shouldered in Berlin by a group of arrogant men in brown shirts who seemed to think that the whole world should stand aside for them. I was a bit perturbed when I saw local people, some of them quite mature, being deliberately pushed aside by these young men in this strange brown uniform. Little did I know the world was heading for its most turbulent period in history.

When Scotland beat Czechoslovakia 3-1 in Prague in 1937, the Press were extremely generous in their praise of the left-wing triangle of George Brown, Bob McPhail and Torry Gillick. Centre-half Jimmy Simpson, Torry and myself, got the goals in a match I thoroughly enjoyed.

In all I played 17 times for Scotland. Five times against England, five times against Northern Ireland, three times against Wales and four times against foreign opposition. I finished on the winning side on 11 occasions, and three times on a losing side. I scored seven goals.

By modern standards it may not seem a lot of caps, but there was no European championship in those days and Britain was not at all interested in the World Cup at that time. So the British countries were restricted to their three internal games each season, plus the odd game now and then against European opposition. I feel now that I got my fair share — even if I never did play at Wembley, and had to pull out of other games. I played with a lot of great players when attendance figures were being smashed almost every season. These were peak years in football and I was just happy to be involved at the highest level.

I may have no memories of Wembley, but my Scottish Cup medals are proving a great comfort!

7

The Ibrox Genius We Called "Mr"

It was 27 October 1928. My head was spinning, but it had nothing to do with playing my first game for Scotland, as a Rangers player, against Wales at Ibrox. I was half fu' and didn't know it!

Just before we went out on to the field before a crowd of 55,000, a Queen's Park official went round the Scottish players with a bottle of "magic potion" encouraging us to have a spoonful, as it would pep us up for the game. I took my "medicine" without hesitation and felt the mixture bite into my tongue and warm my throat as I swallowed it. It turned out to be a powerful mixture of brandy and port, the first time I had ever taken or indeed tasted alcohol. But I didn't know this.

Now this was Scotland's first game after the 5-1 victory over England at Wembley seven months earlier when the legend of the "Wembley Wizards" was born. I was the only forward playing against Wales who hadn't played at Wembley. Alex James was out, I was there in his place. But frankly I wasn't too sure where I was in the first half. I seemed to be playing in a bit of a mist, with my reflexes decidedly suspect.

One man in the stand knew something was very wrong — Bill Struth. When I went into the dressing-room at half-time Struth was already waiting for me. "What's wrong with you?" he asked. Eventually I revealed that I had taken a huge spoon of something out of a bottle just before the game and it had burned my throat a bit.

The Rangers manager quickly found out what had been in the bottle then told me to go into the toilet and stick my finger down my throat. I did as I was told, produced the result that Struth wanted, and was told to go out and play the way he expected me to play.

Things got much better in the second half, when I felt I was really part of a game which we won 4-2. If the brandy and port mixture hadn't done me any favours, it seemed to have the opposite effect on Hughie Gallacher. He scored a first-half hat-trick!

This story illustrates how meticulous Struth was as a manager. He would leave absolutely nothing to chance. He sought answers to everything and would settle for nothing less than perfection. Struth was not prepared to see me, as a Rangers player, struggle my way through an international match. He knew there was something affecting my play and he wanted to find out what it was, and if he could come up with a solution. In this case it was my finger down my throat. But there was no way he would sit back and allow things to drift along. It wasn't his style.

I wonder how many other managers would have acted as Struth did that day? My respect for the man grew after this incident, and it kept on growing until the day he died. There was no better manager in the world of football. He was the best.

Most people already know that Bill Struth had been a professional runner in his early days, running anything from 100 yards to 880 yards. He had done his training at Tynecastle and might well have become a trainer there if Hearts had offered him enough money. They didn't, Clyde did, and he moved to Shawfield as trainer in 1908. Was it just a coincidence that Clyde made the final of the Scottish Cup for the first time in their history two years later? I wonder.

In 1914, at the outbreak of World War 1, Struth became trainer at Ibrox. Six years later, at the age of 43, he became manager, after the tragic death of Willie Wilton, who drowned in a boating accident in Gourock Bay.

Struth's first signing has to be significant. It was Alan Morton, the little Queen's Park outside-left who had already played twice for Scotland. "Mr" Struth, as we all called him at Ibrox, was telling the football public that nothing but the best would do for him at Ibrox. And there wasn't a better left-winger anywhere in the world than this wee man who was to become known throughout football as "the wee blue devil".

In his first season as manager Struth set a League Championship record that still stands to this day. Rangers took 76 points from a possible 84 in a 22-club league. Their only defeat was from Celtic at Ibrox, losing 2-0. Now that Scotland's Premier Division has reverted to just ten clubs with 36 games it looks as though the Struth record of 76 points will stand for all time, unless there is league reconstruction, which seems unlikely.

Those who *thought* they knew Struth would immediately call him a despot, an inflexible dictator, with Victorian standards of discipline, who ruled Ibrox with a rod of iron. Well, of course, he wasn't really like that. I found him a very fair man, and a very understanding man. He had a rigid code of conduct which didn't do any of us any harm. You had to realise that what he did was for the good of Rangers and for yourself.

He never talked about the tactics of football and never ever told you how you should play, or where you should play. You were the professional footballer, so you shouldn't need to be told. His job was to get you fit, motivate you and make you realise the importance of playing for Rangers.

I have no hesitation in saying right here that being a Rangers player under Struth, made me a better human being. The discipline I learned at Ibrox stayed with me for the rest of my life.

Who was it that said you've got to learn to walk before you run? It might have been Bill Struth. Our first chore every day at training at Ibrox was a walk around the track . . . in our suits! When we reported for training at 10.30 a.m. we would take our coats and hats off, and then walk out on to the track with Struth in our normal attire. We would then walk round the track, doing breathing exercises. It would be one lap on a day of poor weather, two laps if the weather was good. The manager would shout out as we walked round the track: "Breathe in deeply, lads, it's good for you." Unfortunately there was an incinerator nearby which occasionally produced the most obnoxious smells and on the bad days Sandy Archibald could be heard to say: "Here we go, breathing in all that shit again!"

Struth seemed oblivious to it and I wasn't prepared to present too many objections, as he always chose to walk alongside me each morning as we strolled round the track in twos. Eventually I asked Struth why he did choose to walk beside me. He replied: "Young man, it is because your stride suits my stride." Nonetheless he walked on the inside of the track. Like the old ped he was, he kept to the inside and made me walk extra yards on the bends.

He didn't waste his time while we walked. He would ask my opinion of certain players and opposing teams and talk on all aspects of the game. I think it was his way of getting second opinions and maybe even the mood of his dressing-room. He was no fool.

Struth hated swearing. He would have none of it in the dressing-room and didn't want to hear it on the field. He was also violently

Bill Struth, the greatest manager of them all, poses, immaculate as ever, beside the portrait presented to him by the civic heads of the city of Glasgow in 1953. A year, appropriately enough, when Rangers had a League and Scottish Cup double.

opposed to smoking, so you daren't be seen with a fag in your hand anywhere near the ground. In these days most of us did smoke. Some more than others.

To the disgust of my fellow smokers at Ibrox I smoked a tipped cigarette called Craven 'A', which prompted Archibald to say: "You'd need a poultice on your neck to get a good draw out of them." It meant that no one wanted to smoke my fags, and I certainly didn't want to smoke the full-strength variety. Though I have long since given up the weed, I did smoke during my playing career, but never before I played.

I would have one last fag around teatime, which was generally 5.30 p.m., and wouldn't "light up" again until after the game the following day. Nor would I go out on a Friday night. I would stay at home and have an early night. I took my football very seriously.

Struth also demanded punctuality. He detested people being late for anything. I learned my lesson at Buchanan Street Station one Saturday when I caught the train to Aberdeen by just four minutes, with Struth standing waiting for me on the platform. I told him I had been late because the Barrhead to Glasgow train had been delayed. He looked at me and said: "Young man, you could have caught an earlier train from Barrhead." I was never late again.

He could be a bit of a fusspot before matches. He would make sure you would be perfectly turned out for every game. He would go round the players buttoning up their shirts, and would make sure that the red at the top of our stockings would be in alignment. The last piece of gear you'd put on would be your white pants. He didn't want to see a smudge on them before you played. He had a phobia about laces breaking during a game. So if you had any doubts about your laces, you threaded in a new set. Struth wanted his players to be like tradesmen. Fully equipped and fully prepared for their job. Faulty equipment, like dodgy laces, could pose problems on the field and Struth demanded that at least we look the part.

I have often thought that Struth busied himself with the players, as I have described, just to fill in the minutes before we were called on to the field. He never did say much before a match, though prior to all the major games like Cup finals, he would say: "Now's the day, now's the hour."

The fact that he'd never kicked a ball in his life and never ever told players how to play, used to intrigue other managers who were themselves former players. I remember clearly the Celtic manager Willie Maley, who was a former player, once asking me what kind of a manager Bill Struth was. I just had to reply that Struth put 100 per cent into being manager of Rangers and expected 100 per cent in return. It was an answer that really didn't satisfy Maley, because he couldn't understand how someone who had never played football could run such a successful club as Rangers.

Of course Struth was very much the psychologist. He had us all running on to the field with a packet of Glucose 'D' tablets in our pockets, telling us to pop one into our mouths when we began to feel tired and this would give us extra strength. I doubt if they did, but we

It's smiles all round as we sharpen up for the start of the 1934-35 season with a bit of running in spiked shoes on the Ibrox track. Skipper Davie Meiklejohn and I set the pace with Jack Drysdale, Dougie Gray, George Brown and Irishman Alex Stevenson looking like extras from the film "Chariots of Fire."

thought they did, and we invariably finished our games strongly.

Our change strip was a white shirt, which we all detested, because they were so damned cold. The air seemed to get inside the shirts and chill the body. When we complained to the manager about the shirts, he promptly opened a bottle of methylated spirits and rubbed our fronts and backs with the stuff. He would then say: "That'll keep the cold out."

I cannot hide the fact that I was a favourite of Bill Struth. While Davie Meiklejohn was the club captain, I was the unofficial vice-captain, and Struth relied heavily on us to make sure the team played the way he wanted. He would have "Meek" upstairs in his office for a chat before most matches. What was said then was not for general consumption, but it was obvious to me that "Meek" would probably be telling Struth how the game should be tackled and where our advantages would be.

I only know that Struth always made a point of telling me before games to "get the whip out" and make sure the forwards were kept on their toes. He was a fair man, but he was cute. If he didn't know too much about football, he knew how to handle men. When he called you upstairs to reprimand you, you could guess his mood instantly. He would address me as "Bob" or "McPhail". If it was "Bob" it was a gentle slap on the wrist. If it was "McPhail" it was a stern warning!

My problem was one of early retaliation. If someone kicked me, then I kicked them back. I believed in an eye for an eye, and opponents soon learned to their discomfort that if they kicked McPhail, then they'd get a bloody sore one in return. Bill Struth did not like my philosophy. He would have me upstairs, give me that piercing look, and tell me: "What you are doing is not good for Rangers. All eyes are on you when you are wearing the jersey. If you are playing the man, then you are not playing the ball and this is what we are paying you to do. If you are fouled then leave things to the referee. You must *not* retaliate." I would promise, of course, to be a good boy, but all my good intentions would go out of the window when I was deliberately fouled by an opponent. They didn't call me "greetin' Boab" for nothing!

There were no secrets from our manager. He seemed to know the movements of every player when they were away from Ibrox. He knew the players who liked a drink and he would let them know he knew. A quiet and sudden "I'm surprised you were seen drinking in that pub" would be put to some unsuspecting player in the dressing-room. His way of saying don't be seen there again.

He was always able to tell me on a Monday whether or not I had been to church at Barrhead. On the first occasion he pulled me up I replied that I hadn't been to church because I had been to Ibrox having treatment to a leg injury. "I can't be in two places at one time, Mr Struth," I replied. He just smiled and turned away. It was some time later that I found out that a church elder in my kirk named James Archibald was a friend of Struth. He was keeping an eye on me on a Sunday morning.

Struth's first love, of course, was athletics, so when he heard that Eric Liddell, who had won the 1924 Olympic 400-metres crown in Paris, would be around Glasgow in 1931 he immediately invited him to come to Ibrox and to do a bit of training. Liddell accepted.

At that time Liddell was on the staff of the Anglo-Chinese College in Tientsin, the city of his birth, carrying out his missionary work. If my memory serves me correctly this was his first visit to Scotland since he left for China in 1925. Struth was a bit apprehensive before Liddell's first visit to Ibrox. We had hardly entered the front door one morning when he was telling us: "Watch your language today. We're having a visit from Eric Liddell."

We were all in some awe of the man when he did turn up. He turned out to be a quiet, polite person who was given the referee's dressing-room to strip in. He smiled easily and was friendly enough, and obviously seemed quite happy to loosen up and do a bit of training round the track.

After a few visits from Liddell we began to get used to his presence and he started doing some sprint training with us. I don't know how the race developed but at one session it was decided that our irrepressible right-winger Sandy Archibald would run against the former Olympic champion over one lap. Was Struth behind it? It wouldn't have surprised me. He just loved to pump some competition into our sprint training.

Now Sandy could run a bit, like an international winger should, and was certainly not short of stamina. To the rest of the players it seemed a waste of time Liddell bothering to take his suit off and change. Well, the race got under way — the full 440 yards — and Archibald won! Chariots of Fire indeed! It was only in the final 15 or 20 yards that Sandy got his nose in front and then won the sprint to the tape. We couldn't believe it. Nor could Struth.

Sandy, brash as ever, said, after recovering his breath: "Next time I run, I'll be really trying!" Liddell just smiled, said "Well done" and went into the referee's room to change.

What the time of the race had been I've no idea but when Liddell had won his Olympic crown seven years earlier he had smashed the world record for 400 metres with a time of 47.6 seconds. Of course he had long since given up competitive running because of his missionary work in China, but he was still only 29 years of age and probably two or three years younger than Archibald.

There was no living with Archibald for weeks after the race, which remarkably was never ever referred to in any newspaper. But he still wasn't the fastest man at Ibrox. I was.

Again Struth was behind the race. He had a fair notion that I could shift over 100 yards — and so had I. A major part of my game was moving quickly with the ball from one side of the field to the other to set up an attack; or else run into the penalty area to meet a cross from Archibald or Morton. A lot of defenders lost a lot of goals over the years because they didn't realise that I was faster than I looked. The ideal opporunity to test my speed came when Struth ran a series of sprints. Eventually I found myself running against a young lad we had signed from Cowdenbeath, Tommy Russell, a left-back, who was to make only a handful of first-time appearances.

This was the final. The 100 yards was paced out, we got on our marks and I won by two or three yards. Even Archibald was surprised that I won. I had, modestly, been quietly confident. Struth positively beamed. He had been right again!

You could never really get close to Struth. He was a man who knew how to keep himself to himself. Though there was a fair bit of vanity in his make-up there was also a lot of understanding and compassion about him which came through eventually. When my father died and was buried at Neilston Cemetery, in Barrhead, I got the surprise of my life to find Struth standing at the graveside to pay his respects. He had not been invited because it was very much a family funeral attended by close friends and near neighbours in Barrhead. But Struth had taken the time to find out where and when my dad was being buried. I thought a lot of him for being there and I like to think it was a compliment to myself.

Struth was very much the father figure to all of us. We were his boys and his job was to make sure he made the most of us. I remember when we were returning from our exhausting 14-match tour of America and Canada in 1930, Struth told us that we were all looking a wee bit "peeky" and that we would have to be built up before we arrived in Glasgow. He immediately cancelled the soup we were getting twice a day and substituted bottles of stout.

Not even the lads who liked a wee drink on the side fancied the taste of stout, and we had every intention of pouring it right over the side of the ship when the bottles were handed out. Struth, though, couldn't be hoodwinked. He stood close at hand when the stout was delivered and stayed with us until we had downed it. It worked. When I was met by my fiancée in Glasgow she looked at me and said: "Nice to see you again, chubby cheeks!"

Struth, who started life as a stonemason, was brought up in the Fountainbridge district of Edinburgh but we soon learned he had been born near Aberdour. Every time we stopped at Milnathort station en route to an away game in that area Struth would shout: "Come on then, lift your hats. This is where I was born!"

No one knew how to get more out of a player than Struth. This was his strength. Regularly he would field big-name players who weren't close to being even 80 per cent fit. He would talk them into playing, knowing that their very presence on the field would worry opponents.

For my part I lost count of the number of games I played when I really should have been sitting up in the stand nursing an injury. I remember Struth taking quite extraordinary steps to keep me playing one season when I was suffering constant pain in my groin. I had been struggling for weeks with the injury when, eventually, Struth arranged for me to see a contact of his.

What the man's medical qualifications were I've never been quite sure, but I finished up in his surgery in the middle of Glasgow, having been driven there by my determined manager. Having got myself stripped and laid out on the treatment table, I was horrified to see the beaming, talkative "practitioner" begin to heat a large needle over what looked like a bunsen burner. Struth smiled encouragingly, as the confident consultant described what he was about to do to me. He was going to heat the tip of the needle, until it was red hot, then jab it into my groin! Apparently this, what seemed to me, barbarous treatment, would eliminate the dead tissue in my groin area and I would soon be as fit as a fiddle. I could feel the perspiration on my forehead and the old knees begin to tremble a bit. Sure enough in went the red-hot needle into my groin area. Was it twice or three times he stuck it into my body? I'm not sure, because I know my eyes were closed — *but, remarkably, I didn't feel a thing.*

Having received a cheerful farewell from this medical man of mystery, the Rangers manager and I set off back to Ibrox. But en route Struth decided he fancied an apple. So he stopped at a fruit shop, left me sitting in the car — and reaction set in. When he returned he must have thought he was looking at a ghost. I had gone chalk white and I just couldn't keep my hands from shaking. He was concerned. He apologised for leaving me in the car alone, said it was thoughtless of him, and quickly took me back to the ground. Though I thought the treatment had been a bit primitive and a bit unnerving, it worked. My fitness improved considerably and of course Bill Struth had come up trumps once more.

Incidentally, I had a quiet smile to myself some time after Graeme Souness arrived as the new manager at Rangers, when I noticed how partial he was to apples. I'm told he's a four apples a day man. I think that was Struth's intake. They've got more in common than you think!

If Graeme is as successful a manager as Struth was he'll have no complaints. In his first 11 years as manager, Struth won the championship nine times. When he retired at the age of 77 in 1954 he had won 18 championships, ten Scottish Cups and the Scottish League Cups of 1947 and 1949. But I've often thought that the matches that gave him most satisfaction were the two meetings with Arsenal in September 1933 to decide the unofficial championship of Great Britain.

8

The Best in Britain — and Arsenal Agree

Herbert Chapman was a showman who gloried in publicity. Everything
about him was flamboyant, even his very gestures. He had a style, vision
and confidence in his own ability to mould winning teams. He made
Arsenal. The London club had done nothing until Chapman burst
through their front doors in 1925 to make them one of the finest clubs
in the world. It was therefore inevitable that Rangers and Arsenal
would meet head on to decide who was Britain's number one.

A moderate player with 'Spurs, Chapman, who had a similar stature
to Alex James — centre parting and well-slicked hair as well — had
already proved himself an outstanding manager. He took over
Huddersfield Town just after the First World War at the age of 45, led
them out of the Second Division — and then into their first ever FA Cup
final in 1920. Under Chapman, Huddersfield became First Division
champions for the first time in 1924 and retained the title in 1925 and
1926, by which time he had taken command of the London "Gunners".

Chapman was a man well ahead of his time. He didn't hesitate to pay
record transfer fees for players, believed in floodlit football, installed a
stadium clock at Highbury, numbered his players, and suggested it was
high time the England international team should meet for regular
training sessions.

Arsenal won their first major trophy in 1930, beating Huddersfield
in the FA Cup final with Alex James, transferred for a Scottish record
fee of £9,000 from Raith Rovers, as their midfield schemer, and David
Jack, transferred for a British record fee of £11,800 at the age of 30
from Bolton, as the inspiration of the attack. When Chapman brought
the championship to Highbury for the first time in 1931 and then again
in 1933, Bill Struth and Chapman decided it was time to organise an
unofficial British championship decider, over two games.

Rangers had just regained the First Division championship by three points from Motherwell. There was a fair bit of fever about. The teams in the first match at Ibrox in September were *Rangers*: Dawson; Gray and McDonald; Meiklejohn, Simpson, Brown; Main, Stevenson, Smith, McPhail, Nicholson. *Arsenal*: Moss; Compton, Hapgood; Hill, Roberts, John; Bowden, Jack, Coleman, James, Bastin.

I knew there would be critical comparison of the play of Alex James and myself. We were both vying for the Scotland inside-left position, and the country seemed split on who should secure the position as their right. James, who had scored two goals for the "Wembley Wizards", had a big support because of his Wembley success, but I had proved myself in four of Scotland's last five games. I was determined to do well.

It was fortunate for Arsenal that their 'keeper Frank Moss had an outstanding game. We looked like burying them. I had an early header which I thought was a scorer, until Moss got his fingers to it and tipped it over the crossbar. We had started well and we didn't let up. It surprised no one that we took the lead in 36 minutes, when our left-winger Willie Nicholson beat Leslie Compton and hit the ball off the post. Jimmy Smith was there to kick it into the net.

Jerry Dawson had one superb save from their left-winger Cliff Bastin before I scored our second goal. Nicholson swept the ball out to Bobby Main who quickly returned to me. I got the ball under control quickly and gave it a good old-fashioned thumping into the net. A goal I was very pleased about. So we won 2-0, though it should have been more.

The Press were good to me. I was purring like a cat when I read the following morning: "This was the finest exhibition from McPhail since he came into football."

Wee Alex and I had a good old chin-wag after the game, with most of the questions coming from him. He was a great fellow for analysing everyone's game. He asked me about the goal I had scored against them. How much time did I have to control the ball? What was I thinking when I got the ball? Did I pick my spot to score? Could Arsenal have prevented it? He had a very active, inquiring mind and was always seeking opinions, ideas and thoughts from opponents or team-mates.

I had a great admiration for this wee man, who was only five feet five inches in height. He was a great manipulator of the ball, had superb control and gave great thought to everything he was doing on the field. He didn't try to run a lot. With his skill he didn't have to. When he played, Arsenal played, and that was often!

I have to make some mention of David Jack, the Arsenal inside-right. According to modern regulations he would have been considered eligible for Scotland. His father was a Scot who had played for Alloa. I recall him as the Plymouth Argyle manager and indeed David played with his dad's club before moving to Bolton. This is where he made his reputation.

In 1923 he went into the history books as the first player to score at Wembley. This was in the FA Cup final when he scored the first goal for Bolton in a 2-0 win over West Ham — a remarkable occasion, because a record 126,047 paid to get into the first Wembley final while another 70,000 broke in! Not surprisingly there were all kinds of crowd problems, with the kick-off delayed by 40 minutes.

Jack was back at Wembley with Bolton three years later and scored the only goal in the victory over Manchester City. When he joined Arsenal two years later he became the first player to be transferred for five figures. A tall, slender figure, I remember him as a beautifully balanced player, who was prepared to take on an entire defence and expected to beat them.

If we had played well at Ibrox, we were positively brilliant in the second leg at Highbury, and I'm being a bit modest in saying that. The teams seven days later were — *Rangers*: Dawson; Gray, McDonald; Meiklejohn, Simpson, Brown; Archibald, Marshall, Smith, McPhail, Fleming. *Arsenal*: Moss; Male, Hapgood; Hill, Roberts, John; Birkett, Bowden, Lambert, James, Bastin.

We knew that wee Alex would be out to take control of the game, show us all of his tricks and send us home with our tails between our legs. So we discussed how we should tackle the game. Eventually Davie Meiklejohn said: "Just leave James to me."

There were 40,000 in the Arsenal ground and they got real value for money — from Rangers. However, "Meek's" plans didn't seem to be working too well when James cleverly sent Jack Lambert, their centre-forward, through to score in 25 minutes. But we really shouldn't have had any doubts. In the 42nd minute Doc Marshall scored what was perhaps the most electrifying goal of his career. He took a superbly timed pass from George Brown on the run, and without a break in stride, hammered the ball from long range past the startled Frank Moss. Because it was a hazy day of indifferent visibility most of the crowd didn't realise the ball was in the net until they saw the 'keeper digging it out.

*My great contemporary and rival, Alex James, shows off the FA Cup after skippering
Arsenal to a 1-0 win over Sheffield United at Wembley in 1936.*

Jimmy Smith didn't know it, but he had broken a toe in the first half after a rough tackle by Harry Roberts. Smithie decided to stay on the field and moved to outside-left in the second half. This allowed Jimmy Fleming to return to his favourite position at centre-forward. Within a minute of the restart "Flem" scored with a header from a typical Sandy Archibald cannonball corner and then put us in the lead with another good goal just minutes later. It was lame-duck Smithie who gave him a neat little through pass which allowed "Flem" to run past George Male and whip the ball low into the net. We had won 3-1. I doubt if any of us had put so much effort into any game. I clearly remember Archibald saying in the dressing-room: "I've never been in such a state of exhaustion before."

The most frustrated man on the field was Alex James. Every time he took possession he would look up expecting to be tackled. Instead Meiklejohn, his marker, stayed clear of him and was quite content to jockey him. Eventually Alex started shouting: "Come and get it! Come on . . . what's keeping you? Is no one coming to tackle me?"

Well, of course, this wee man was a master at slipping a tackle, and making the space for his passes to the dangerous Cliff Bastin down the left wing. "Meek" simply tied him up by forcing him to make passes he didn't want to make. An agressive player by nature, "Meek" outwitted him by refusing to make any kind of tackle on him while he was operating so deep in the midfield.

The crowd was tremendous. We were cheered off the field for our efforts. A Sunday newspaper wrote: "Rangers served up a class of football which has not been seen from an English club this generation. There is probably no English club capable of playing this delectable type of soccer." This man knew his football! A gracious Arsenal director said in our dressing-room: "On the form you showed today you are good enough to beat England." You know I thought we had. The following season Arsenal had seven players in the England side which beat Italy 3-2 at Highbury . . . and they didn't have the services of Alex James.

The double victory over Arsenal proved a lot to us. We had beaten the best in Britain with a fair bit to spare. George Male and Eddie Hapgood were to become the permanent England full-backs; Cliff Bastin had just scored 33 league goals in 42 games, which is still an English record for a winger; Ray Bowden, who replaced David Jack, went on to play six times for England; their 'keeper Frank Moss played for England as did their centre-half Harry Roberts. Left-half Bob

John, who was to play 422 league games for Arsenal, was a tenacious player who worked well with James on the left side of the field. Overall, Arsenal were an outstanding side. They won the championship again that season, and completed the hat-trick in 1935. So we were justified in taking a lot of pride from these victories.

But all of us were quite sad when Chapman, who had played golf with Bill Struth at Turnberry prior to the Ibrox game, died suddenly in January 1934 at the age of 61. He has to be remembered as one of the greatest managers of all time, and as the man who created one of the most successful sides in the history of British football.

There is little doubt in my mind that the goal scored by "Doc" Marshall in that Highbury match got him a transfer to Arsenal in July the following year. While at Ibrox he was offered a medical post in London, which he talked over with Bill Struth. When it became apparent Jimmy was keen to take it, the transfer was arranged. Unfortunately he didn't have the same success at Highbury as he had at Ibrox.

On the morning of the Highbury match I learned I had been named as captain and inside-left of the Scotland team to meet Wales at Cardiff on 4 October. This pepped me up considerably. But not for the first time I had to pull out of the international match because of injury. So I lost the only chance I had of playing alongside Matt Busby in a Scotland jersey. Matt from Bellshill, and later of course to become creator and guru of Manchester United, was then playing for Manchester City. Surprisingly this was the only full cap he ever got, though he did play in seven wartime internationals. Jimmy Easson of Portsmouth took my place. Wales won 3-2 and Scotland's scorers were Dally Duncan and Willie McFadyen.

I was, however, fit to play against Partick Thistle on the Saturday when a young lad named Torry Gillick made his debut as my left-winger partner. Torry was a good player, smart off his mark, and easy to play with. If my memory serves me right he was the only player that Struth ever transferred — to Everton — and then bought back.

The matches with Arsenal of course developed into an annual affair, because they proved to be entertaining and highly competitive. My last game against the London club was in August 1938 when two players made their Rangers debuts — Willie Waddell and Jock Shaw. Our team that day was: Dawson; Gray, Shaw; McKillop, Simpson, Brown; Waddell, Fiddes, Smith, McPhail and Kinnear.

The attendance was 39,400 and I think a large section of the crowd was there to see Arsenal's new signing Bryn Jones, who had just been transferred from Wolves for a British record transfer fee of £14,000. Though signed as an inside-forward, the Welshman was fielded at outside-right that day. But not for long. He finished the game in his normal position. I was delighted to read the comment of one scribe after the match: "If Jones is worth £14,000 then McPhail is worth the Bank of England." A wee bit unfair on Jones, I thought. It's never easy trying to live up to a record transfer fee in your first game away from home. However I did enjoy the game.

Waddell, who was to become the Rangers manager many years later and who was to guide them to the European Cup Winners Cup victory in Barcelona in 1972, could only have been about 16 when he made his debut. Because I was very much a senior player by this time, I had a word with the young Willie Waddell before the game. I told him that I realised it was a big occasion for him and advised him to use his natural speed to get down the wing and hit crosses to the far post. His major asset at that age was his speed and I told him to make the most of it.

I knew he had two good feet and could cross the ball well with either. But I suggested he concentrate on hitting the ball across with his right foot to get the natural loop which would carry the ball away from the 'keeper. If he crossed with his left foot then the natural curve of the ball would carry the ball into the 'keeper's hands.

He listened and he played very well considering his age. Indeed he couldn't have made a better debut, because he scored the only goal of the game! He got it somewhere in the middle of the first half, when he decided to have a go himself, hit the 'keeper, and then thumped the rebound into the net. As I recall he almost got a second goal late in that first half.

Shaw was a much more experienced player, having been transferred from Airdrie the previous season and already capped by the Scottish league. Because of his never-say-die spirit, the fans were soon calling him "Tiger" and there wasn't a prouder man in the world than Jock when he skippered Rangers to three successive Scottish Cup wins in 1948, 1949 and 1950.

When Waddell came into the Rangers side the war drums were already being heard and I was in my last full season with the club. But I played with him on many occasions. One I recall vividly, because he was my left-wing partner. It was against Kilmarnock at Rugby Park — and I was damned if I could find him. In the course of the game I said to him: "Look, son, I'm having difficulty in finding you." He replied:

"Don't worry about me, I'm watching this right-back." I quickly told him that he shouldn't be worrying about the right-back and that the back should be worrying about him. I said: "You're putting yourself out of the game. You come back from him and let me see you." He did. I sent him the passes and he did well after that. His ability to hit the ball across with his left foot, made him very effective.

I knew in these early days that Struth would like him. He was big, he was strong and he could run. And he wasn't afraid of anything. In that first season Willie actually played more league games than I did, scoring seven goals in 27 games. And he won his first championship medal — as did our bright new centre-forward Willie Thornton.

Willie, who had joined us the previous season, scored 23 goals in 35 league games. How many did he score with his head from Waddell crosses? I wonder! In the years to follow this telepathic partnership was to prove one of Rangers' most devastating assets.

9

I Equal McMenemy's Scottish Cup Record

If ever a player deserved to lead a Rangers team to a Scottish Cup win it was Horace. He was a gifted player with a great confidence in his own ability who revelled in responsibility, and never ever let us forget that we were most fortunate to be allowed to play for Rangers.

Tommy Muirhead had been given the dressing-room nickname of Horace because he actually suited a bowler hat, was most meticulous about his clothes and was the only member of the team to wear spats. He was a bit of a dandy, I suppose, and felt that he was a bit above the rest of the lads because he worked hard on good manners. He also happened to be a bloody good captain.

Horace, who had joined Rangers from Hibs for a mere £20 in 1917, must go into the record book as the bargain buy of all time. Nowadays he would be referred to as a midfielder. Then he was an inside-forward converted to half-back, mostly left-half. He played directly behind me in many of my early games at Ibrox, so I came to know the man as a clever footballer who could tackle like a tiger and pass the ball with stunning accuracy.

He had, unfortunately, missed the emotional 1928 Scottish Cup win against Celtic because of an injury to a knee. But he led us out in the 1929 final against Kilmarnock before another bumper Hampden crowd of 114,708. It seemed that all we had to do was throw a set of Rangers strips on to the field and the Cup would be ours. We should have known better. The only change in the side which had won the Cup the previous year was Muirhead for Andy Cunningham at inside-right. Killie were a young side, supposedly signed for a total of £800.

After only 15 minutes Rangers were awarded a penalty kick when big Jock Buchanan was pulled down as he seemed to be going through to score. Debate! Referee Tom Dougray, who was never particularly friendly to myself or Davie Meiklejohn, because we moaned a lot, gave the kick, then changed his mind twice. Kilmarnock persuaded him to consult one linesman, which he did. He then decided that it wasn't a penalty and that the game should be restarted by dropping the ball. This we didn't fancy at all, so we asked him to consult the other linesman. It *was* a penalty kick after all.

"Meek" had taken the historic kick in the 1928 final. This time it was up to Tully Craig, our left-half. Tully hit the kick well, but Sam Clemie in the Killie goal brought off a tremendous save — and that gave the Ayrshire side a lot of heart. I had a good scoring chance just before the interval but I hit the ball too early and sent it wide of the post. This got a great cheer from the Killie fans who didn't like me too much. Because my brother Malcolm had played with Killie and had won a medal with them in 1920, I always tried to play well at Rugby Park and show off a bit. Another reason why I always wanted to play well against them was that I had played a trial for them before I had joined Airdrie, and had played a stinker. They didn't ask me back. I think I was trying to prove they had made a dreadful mistake.

Just after the interval we knew we were in trouble when we lost a goal to their left-winger John Aitken. Hughie Morton, the Killie right-half, sent in an awkward lob which caught Tom Hamilton slightly off-balance. Instead of diving at the ball he kicked it away — straight to Aitken's feet. He hit it in his stride into the back of the net. Then in 73 minutes Jimmy Williamson got a second goal for Kilmarnock when he cleverly hooked a corner kick from Connell on the right into the roof of our net. After that Killie looked more like scoring than we did.

We were beaten, but more drama was to follow. Jock Buchanan, who had been brought to the club as a cover for the injury-prone Muirhead, was sent off. He had, not for the first time, lost his temper and told referee Dougray what he thought of him. He became the first player to be sent off in a Cup final this century. It was another 55 years before another player was sent off in a Scottish Cup final and that was Roy Aitken of Celtic after a wild tackle on Mark McGhee of Aberdeen. Roy might like to know that in comparison to Jock, with whom I used to share a room on my early trips with Rangers, he can be considered gentle!

Muirhead didn't know it, but that was his last chance of winning a Scottish Cup medal. He never did play in another final. Having beaten Kilmarnock home and away in the league we just couldn't believe we could play so badly in a final. We simply deserved to lose to a better side on the day. I didn't enjoy the experience one little bit. Horace would just have loved to dangle a Scottish Cup medal on his watch chain. But it wasn't to be.

I think I should mention that most of the Rangers players had nicknames before I arrived at Ibrox, so it took me a wee while to get used to the strange names being shouted around me during my early games. They certainly confused opponents at times and, maybe more importantly, referees.

I think I've already mentioned that our 'keeper Tom Hamilton was known as "the Drummer". Our left-back Bob Hamilton was called "Newry" because that was the part of Ireland where he was born. Jimmy Simpson was called "Scrapings", Meiklejohn was, of course, "Meek" and George Brown was "Brownie". Wee Alan Morton was "Pinkie" because of his size, Sandy Archibald was "Harry", Tommy Craig was "Tully", Billy McCandless was "Bucksie" and Jimmy Fleming was "Flem". Big Bob McAulay revelled in being called "Al Capone" simply because he had lived in America during the reign of this particular Chicago gangster.

It was Mattha Gemmell, the Clyde trainer, who got me the nickname of "Whistle". After a game against Clyde at Shawfield, I had come out of the bath and was drying myself, when Mattha came in. He looked at the McPhail body, which didn't have too much meat on it, and said: "My goad Boab, if you bored a few holes on that boady 'o yours you'd look like a whistle." The name stuck.

One nickname that tickled me immensely was that given to big Neilly Dewar of Third Lanark. He was called "Silver sleeves". Why? Because he had a habit of wiping his nose with the sleeves of his jersey!

"Whistle" McPhail found himself back in the Scottish Cup final for a third successive year in 1930. The opposition this time was Partick Thistle, who had beaten Rangers in the 1921 final, and I was to face a little terrier-like opponent called Alex Elliott who was a pain in the backside to me. I never ever played a good game against him. He used to stick to me like a limpet mine. No matter what I did in any game against the Jags, this wee pest Elliot was always there. For some reason or other he seemed to produce his best form against Rangers, and me in particular. But he was fair . . . and he could tackle!

Sadly Horace, or should I say Muirhead, again wasn't fit to play. I think he was again recovering from yet another cartilage operation, the third in his career. In his last season at Rangers I used to look at his knees and wonder how he could walk, never mind play. His legs looked

Two of Arsenal's greatest-ever forwards, Alex James and David Jack, getting in some golf during a close season holiday in South Devon, along with a friend.

gey shaky to me. His replacement was again that bold buccaneer Jock Buchanan. Out too was wee Alan, who had been injured in the 5-2 defeat from England at Wembley where Jimmy Fleming had scored both Scotland's goals. I might add that Buchanan was also in that Scotland team, to gain the second of his two caps, which proved how good a player he was, even though Bill Struth had signed him as an experienced cover for Muirhead.

I'm afraid the 107,425 crowd didn't get a lot for their money. The match finished a goal-less draw and I rarely got a kick at the ball. In the replay Morton was fit enough to replace Willie Nicholson on the left wing, and Struth decided to pull in Bob "Whitey" McDonald in place of Buchanan. Why? There was some doubt about Jock's fitness but I had the feeling that our manager was also just a wee bit worried about his temperament, and in pulling in "Whitey" he really wasn't taking any risks.

Though he had been born in Belfast, and indeed played twice for Northern Ireland, "Whitey" had been discovered during our 1928 close-season tour of the USA and Canada. He had played well against us in one of our Canadian matches, when he revealed himself as one of the longest throwers of a ball I'd ever seen. Struth was certainly impressed. "Whitey's" throw-ins were as good as any corner-kick or free-kick, and he also happened to be a very good player. One of the best goals I ever scored came from one of his throws against Ayr United at Somerset Park. At that time he was still catching out opponents with his long throws, because he wasn't too well known. But I knew what to expect and I got myself to the edge of the penalty box for one of his missile-like throws. It was perfect. I hit the ball as it dropped and almost burst the Ayr net. It was a goal I've never forgotten . . . but to this day I'm damned if I can remember whether or not we won that game.

So for the final replay the teams were — Rangers: T. Hamilton; Gray, R. Hamilton; McDonald, Meiklejohn, Craig; Archibald, Marshall, Fleming, McPhail and Morton. Partick Thistle: Jackson; Calderwood, Rae; Elliott, Lambie, McLeod; Ness, Grove, Boardman, Ballantyne and Torbet. This time 104,000 turned up at Hampden on the Wednesday which meant that Rangers had become the first club in history to play before 500,000 spectators in the Scottish Cup in a season. Eat your heart out, Graeme Souness!

Within 15 minutes Alan Morton was hobbling. A recurrence of the Wembley injury or a fresh groin strain? I don't know, but I do know that for the rest of the match he limped up and down the wing trying to make himself available to touch on the ball if I was looking for a quick return pass. In these days there were no substitutes, so the injury to Morton was a serious blow to us. As it turned out, it was to be wee "Pinkie's" last final. He was now 37 and though he continued to play off and on for the next three seasons, his best days were over. When he retired as a player he immediately became a director of the club. Then he became "Mr" Morton, but he was always Alan to me.

"Whitey" McDonald had settled into the game extremely well and it was his cross in the 41st minute that gave us the half-time lead. "Doc" Marshall hit the cross first time against Alex Lambie, but followed up well to beat Johnny Jackson on his left side.

With Elliott always on top of me and having no winger to hit passes at, I wasn't having one of my better days. When Johnny Torbet got the Thistle's equaliser in the 71st minute I thought, "Things are not looking good." However five minutes from the end Tully Craig, who had missed the vital penalty in the previous final, made amends. He met a clearance from Lambie some 25 yards out and lobbed it at the Thistle goal. Jackson, with the sun in his eyes, made a frantic effort to get his hands to it, failed, and the ball finished in the net. I had just won my third Scottish Cup medal.

The Partick Thistle chairman Tom Reid produced a laugh when he said: "We played well but the only consolation for us is that we held the Scottish team to a goal." When you look at the Rangers team he wasn't far wrong.

That victory crowned a remarkable season for Rangers. They had become the first club to win everything they had competed in. They won the Scottish Cup, the Glasgow Cup, the Glasgow Charity Cup, the League Championship, the Second XI Cup and the Alliance Championship — what is known as "the clean sweep". We had beaten Celtic home and away in the league, whacked them 4-0 in the final of the Glasgow Cup and beat them in the final of the Charity Cup by the toss of a coin — Jimmy McStay guessed wrongly — after we were level on goals and corner-kicks in extra time.

It was a season when Rangers proved you needed a strong pool of players if you were to have any chance of winning every available trophy. When we beat Celtic 1-0 in a league match that season we were without Dougie Gray, Tully Craig, Tommy Muirhead and Alan Morton, who were playing for Scotland at Wales, and Bob Hamilton, Davie Meiklejohn and Jock Buchanan who were injured. It was Bob McPhail and the reserves who won that day, with Willie Nicholson getting the winner. When the others returned I was delighted to tell them that they hadn't been missed!

Our 1932 final again went to a replay. For the second time in three years we faced Kilmarnock, so we were determined we would not falter this time. On the Saturday a crowd of 112,000 saw Bud Maxwell give Kilmarnock a half-time lead but just after the interval I got the equaliser and this put us into a Wednesday replay.

This time the crowd was 105,000. There were never any doubts about the winners of the replay. Jimmy Fleming put us ahead in 11 minutes, I scored in the 69th minute and Sam English, who had come through the most traumatic year of his life, scored a third goal with a superb header from a Davie Meiklejohn free-kick. Fleming had replaced the injured Alan Morton, and I remember thinking that our full-backs Dougie Gray and Bob McAulay had been quite outstanding throughout.

My direct opponent in that final and in the 1929 final, which we had lost, was Hughie Morton, a real competitor. He had no love of me because I could always give as good as I took. I recall a friend of mine telling me that Morton had been letting it be known that he would "sort McPhail out" the next time we met, which happened to be that 1929 final. Struth immediately passed this information on to the referee of the day, Tom Dougray, that Morton might cause him a bit of trouble with some heavy treatment of the Rangers inside-left. In his own quiet way Dougray singled out Morton before the final and warned him he'd be watching him extremely closely. Hughie got the message *and* his winner's medal in 1929 and learned that if you concentrate on your game things have a habit of falling into place.

Although Morton and I had to have treatment after a 50-50 tackle for a ball in the 1932 final there was never any vendetta between us. The teams in that final were — *Rangers*: T. Hamilton; Gray, McAulay; Meiklejohn, Simpson, Brown; Archibald, Marshall, English, McPhail, and Fleming. *Kilmarnock*: Bell; Leslie, Nibloe; Morton, Smith, McEwan; Connell, Muir, Maxwell, Duncan, and Aitken.

Our route to our 1934 Cup final win over St Mirren began in quite spectacular fashion. We beat Blairgowrie 14-2 at Ibrox in the first round and Jimmy Fleming scored nine of them. This is still a club record for the number of goals scored by any Rangers player in a single game. Jimmy scored four in the first half, when Rangers led 5-0 and of course five in the second half. "Doc" Marshall got two, Willie Nicholson got one in the first half, and Alex Venters, who had just joined us from Cowdenbeath scored two.

I didn't score any, because I wasn't playing! I watched it all from the stand simply because when Bill Struth felt we faced a bit of easy opposition he would "rest" one or two of his regulars and blood younger players. I was "rested" and was ominously impressed by the wee dark-haired lad who had been bought as my deputy. I later learned that Venters had gone to Struth after a month or so with the club, to express his doubts that he'd ever make it with Rangers. Struth told him: "Young man, you carry on. We'll tell you if we are not pleased." Alex developed into one of the finest inside-forwards in our game.

This was a very special season for me as I was now a married man. I married Jessie Anderson Richmond on 20 June 1933 after a courtship of almost four years. We both came from Barrhead, had gone to the nearby Grahamston School, and Jessie's family lived near the McPhails. She was never really a football fan until we got "serious". So in the final against St Mirren at Hampden there was a very special lady in the stand among the crowd of 113,403.

It turned out to be the easiest final I ever played in. Rangers crushed St Mirren 5-0 and it might have been ten. The personal drama for me came before the game when there was a doubt about me playing. My groin was giving me a lot of trouble and I reported this to Bill Struth. He immediately told the trainer to bandage the upper part of my thigh and the lower part of my body. I said to Struth: "But this bandage will make it very difficult for me to lift my leg." Said Struth: "That may be so, but St Mirren don't know that!"

Now Saints hadn't had a good season. We had beaten them home and away in the league, and they had finished well down the league with only nine wins in 38 games. Yet we were reading stories in the newspapers that the Paisley team were confident they could win and were even talking about winning by at least two goals. Maybe they were trying to convince themselves. But on the day they were a catastrophic flop. Willie Nicholson scored twice, I got a goal in the first half, and wee Bobby Main and Jimmy Smith got the others. It was hard to understand how Saints had beaten Celtic and Motherwell on their way to Hampden. Tom Hamilton made one of the finest saves of his career when the score was 5-0, when he held a tremendous shot from their left-half Miller. I don't think the papers bothered to mention it. On any other occasion it might have earned a headline.

The game in some ways was a triumph for wee Bobby Main, who had been signed five years previously as the replacement for Sandy Archibald. When he arrived at Ibrox we took one look at his wee skinny body — he was less than five feet eight inches tall — and called him "Skin". You had to be someone to get a nickname at Ibrox. He gave the St Mirren left-back Bobby Ancell, the man responsible for the great Motherwell side of the late 1950s, a real hard time of it, and I was delighted to see him get his name on the scoring list when he belted the third goal past McCloy from a crisp pass from "Doc" Marshall. The teams were — *Rangers*: T. Hamilton; Gray, McDonald; Meiklejohn, Simpson, Brown; Main, Marshall, Smith, McPhail and Nicholson. *St Mirren*: McCloy; May, Ancell; Gebbie, Wilson, Miller; Knox, Latimer, McGregor, McCabe and Phillips.

Big Jimmy Smith was our match-winner against Hamilton Accies in the 1935 final which was the first time Rangers had successfully defended the Cup this century. It was a wee bit special to me because it was the one and only time I captained a Rangers team in a final, and thankfully we won it.

It might have been a little embarrassing, personally, if we had lost this final — because I missed a penalty kick, before a goal had been scored. With no Davie Meiklejohn around to give a repeat of his 1928 spot-kick, it fell upon me to take the penalty kick awarded early in the first half when Alex Venters was fouled in the box.

The Accies 'keeper turned out to be the kid next door. I really mean it. He was Jimmy Morgan, who had been pulled in at the last minute to replace the injured Peter Shevlin, the former Celtic 'keeper, and Jimmy had been a next-door neighbour of mine in Barrhead.

With a crowd of 87,286 watching, I gave the kick all I had with my right foot, but sent it just a little too straight. Morgan blocked it, but couldn't hold it. I followed up with another shot and didn't Morgan produce a tremendous save by fisting the ball clear!

Morgan had the game of his life thereafter, but in the 37th minute Jimmy Smith put us ahead. Under some pressure Morgan again fisted a shot clear, but the ball went straight to George Brown. Quickly Brownie whipped the ball low into the goal area, where Smith stuck out his left leg and just managed to get it over the line before the Accies right-back arrived.

I felt a little better after that, though in fairness I thought we had the edge on play. Four minutes after the interval the Accies forwards produced a really smart equaliser, when Davie Wilson headed out to Jimmy King who returned the ball with his head, to give Bert Harrison an opening to score with his head.

But it was the head of Smithie that won us the Cup. From a Torry

Gillick corner on the left in the 61st minute, Smith jumped so well he actually headed the ball down into the net. A tremendous effort.

It had been heavy going throughout the game, with heavy rain and a sodden pitch, and was voted one of the best Cup finals for many years. Accies had played well, but just not well enough, though young Morgan had pulled off a number of good saves, including that penalty kick of mine. I had played perhaps a bit too deep at times during the game, but when I went up into attack I thoroughly enjoyed my forays with the Accies right-half Jackie Cox, who became manager of St Mirren after the war.

I think I should give you that Accies team which was packed with characters, because it was the last time this club appeared in a Scottish Cup final!

Accies: Morgan; Wallace, Bulloch; Cox, McStay, Murray; King, McLaren, Wilson, Harrison, Reid.

Yes the centre-half was Jimmy McStay, the former Celtic skipper, and I have to admit that Jimmy gave a really stuffy performance that day even though our centre-forward Jimmy Smith was the match-winner with his two goals.

I'll never forget the first time I played against Jackie Cox. I had got the better of him in a dribble somewhere in the middle of the field. As I ran past him he tripped me up, quite deliberately, and sent me flying on my face. I got up and snapped at him: "What the hell do you think you're playing at?" With the innocence of a young player he replied: "I was told that if you got the ball past me, then I wasn't to let you past!" What could I say? We became good friends after that little incident and we chuckled over it for years later.

Jimmy Kennedy, who had been signed from Falkirk, had taken over from the injured Meiklejohn at right-half to get his first Cup medal along with Venters, Gillick and 'keeper Jerry Dawson, who would have played in the previous final but for an illness.

Though Jerry was one of the game's greatest-ever 'keepers his goal-kicking was a nightmare. He would insist on taking a semi-circular run at the ball, sometimes from way behind the goal-nets. When the ball came out to you there was so much spin on it that it was almost impossible to "kill" it, or even get anywhere near controlling it. If you went for it with your head, it was liable to go anywhere. We got to the stage of pleading with Jerry to try and kick the ball out straight — but he never did.

Gillick? Now there was some character. He lived in Alan Morton

Arsenal skipper Alex James seems more interested in the lady than the photographer, as we get together after a Film Premier in Glasgow. No mistaking the lads on the left is there? Glasgow's greatest-ever fighter, Benny Lynch and the "mighty atom" from Pontypridd, Jimmy Wilde, former world fly-weight champions. Like me the lads were more interested in our £5 appearance money than the unknown actress!

territory, Airdrie, and he hated wearing a bowler hat. "Torry", his proper name was Terence, would wear a bunnet all the way from his home in Airdrie to Glasgow on match days and then to the far end of Edmiston Drive. He would then stuff his bunnet in his pocket and don the bowler for the walk to Ibrox. What he didn't realise was that Bill Struth had a top flat near Ibrox and he used to watch the lads walking along towards the ground. He quickly spotted "Torry" producing his bowler hat for the last few yards towards the ground. Struth was not amused, and Gillick was quickly paraded upstairs and told what was expected of him as a Rangers player. The bowler hat, particularly on match days, was mandatory.

It was after this final that Struth realised, as I had, that being captain of the side affected my game. I simply tried to do too much because of the responsibility. In that final against Accies I had spent far too much time back helping our defence, playing almost like a fourth half-back. I had no ambition to be captain, so I was delighted when Struth decided that I should concentrate on playing my own game and let someone else take over. Mind you, I did enjoy being captain of a Cup-winning side.

Our 1-0 win over Third Lanark in the 1936 final at Hampden was the first time in the club's history they had achieved a hat-trick of Scottish Cup wins. There were 88,859 spectators at the game and they all left the ground singing the praises of Jerry Dawson. I remember one save he had from the Thirds inside-left Kennedy that was quite spectacular. How he got his hands to the shot through a crowded penalty area I'll never know, but he saved us.

I had now played in seven Scottish Cup-winning sides, and was never again to play in another final. I had therefore equalled Jimmy McMenemy's record number of Cup medals. He had won six with Celtic from 1904 to 1914 and another with Partick Thistle in 1921, at the age of 40. I was fortunate to be part of one of the greatest Rangers squads of this century. Maybe it was the best.

In all I played in eight Scottish Cup finals, including two midweek replays. The total number of spectators who attended these games was a remarkable 1,009,327. When you played with Rangers you learned very early in your career not to be afraid of big crowds!

10

The Celtic Player Who Was My Boyhood Idol

My idol as a kid in Barrhead was a Celtic player. He was Tommy McInally who lived in the village, and who scored 39 goals in his first season at Parkhead in 1919. When I saw him on the street or travelled on the same tram car I would look at him in awe. One day he ruffled my hair as he walked past me and said: "And how's young McPhail?" I was speechless. He knew my name!

If I was at an impressionable age, I don't apologise for it. There are little things in life that somehow stick in your mind forever. I still remember to this day when the great Tommy McInally paid my tram fare. I was now serving my time as a moulder at Cochrane's Foundry, which was in Barrhead. I was heading towards my job. Tommy had come off the train from Glasgow at Barrhead and was taking the tram towards his home in Paisley Road. He saw me on the tram, sat beside me, and promtly paid my fare, which was then three ha'pence, which is worth less than a penny in today's money. It was an instinctive gesture I have never forgotten, and proved to be so typical of this marvellous footballer who laughed and joked his way through his career.

In these early days Tommy was tall and slim and a prolific scorer. In his latter days he was overweight, but a masterly inside-forward, with deft creative touches, which made him one of the best play-makers in the game. Indeed his extra weight proved an advantage, for he was quite brilliant at shielding the ball as he balanced himself to make a telling pass.

As I matured and moved from Pollok Juniors to Airdrie I played against him during the brief period he was with Third Lanark (he was transferred in 1922 over a wage dispute, but returned to Celtic in 1925) and in his latter days at Parkhead, when I was with Rangers.

The stories of Tommy were many. He had a sharp wit and a superb sense of repartee. He liked a wee drink and sometimes he enjoyed several wee drinks which did nothing for the tolerance of his manager, Willie Maley. I enjoyed the story of an angry Maley chastising him for being spotted in a pub prior to a game. Maley said: "You were seen coming out of a public house at half past nine last night. Is that true?" Tommy replied: "Aye, that's right, boss. I couldnae stay any longer, because they were closing!" Maley had no answer to that.

Tommy just wouldn't take himself or the game seriously, despite the efforts of Maley who had brought him back to Celtic Park to replace the great Patsy Gallacher when he moved on to Falkirk. Maley loved McInally — but he was scared to admit it, and time and time again he would overlook his indiscretions.

For years we were constant companions on the 9.39 a.m. train from Barrhead to Glasgow and the 12.35 p.m. train from Glasgow's St Enoch Station to Barrhead. Our regular companions were the Celtic right-half Peter Wilson, the Hearts centre-half Johnny Johnstone, who came from Beith, and that legendary "Red Clydesider" Jimmy Maxton, MP for Bridgeton.

I think it was Johnstone, who was a big, quiet lad, who told me about Tommy's verbal battle with one of the Hearts defenders during a match at Tynecastle. The Hearts player had shouted at Tommy: "Hey, you think you're a great player, don't ye? Well I could eat ye." To which the sharp-witted Thomas replied: "That's the only way you're going to get any fitba' intae you!"

Wilson, who was to play 11 seasons for Celtic and who won four Scottish Cup medals, was a player who knew about economy of movement. In "Old Firm" games he was my direct opponent. He was stylish, had good control and wasted no time in pushing the ball to Pat Connolly on the right wing, Patsy Gallacher and later Alex Thomson in front of him and of course Tommy, who became an inside-left, like myself. But he was quiet compared with Tommy, who so revelled in argument and banter with Jimmy Maxton on our train journeys.

Our group became so well known to rail officials that when we approached the train porters would shout: "Second carriage!" When Maxton, McInally and I boarded at Barrhead, we could always see Peter Wilson hanging out of a window shouting: "In here!"

Now, as a young footballer I knew nothing about politics but I used to listen avidly to Maxton, who was a sick-looking man with long, dark, dank hair and whose shirts always looked as though they'd be none the worse of a good wash. I liked him. He had a keen sense of humour and

107

coped easily with the barbs from McInally, who would keep us all going with his patter.

I suppose we players were more working-class than Jimmy, considering he had attended Hutcheson's Grammar School and Glasgow University where he had graduated as a school teacher. But of course he was very much the left-wing militant, and as leader of the Independent Labour Party, was a fiery advocate of unpopular causes like pacifism and republicanism. I was surprised to learn that he had been thrown in jail in 1915 for sedition, because of his anti-war beliefs, and had had to find labouring jobs when released because no one would give him a job as a teacher.

He was a wonderful speaker and I never doubted the sincerity of the man. He never really went heavily into politics when he travelled with us, but he really did care about men standing around street corners without a job, the people who lived in the rat-infested slums in Glasgow, and the number of people who died of tuberculosis.

At times he looked so ill that I felt quite sorry for him. I've never been quite sure if Jimmy Maxton, in a subtle way, helped me to improve myself as a human being. He certainly caused me to think how lucky I was to make a good living as a professional footballer in those depressed days. The man always seemed to have a great deal more worries than I had. Tommy, of course, never seemed to have any!

Tommy, for all his faults, didn't swear. In all the years I knew him as a train companion, an opponent or a friend sharing a poke of chips at Dougie's Fish Shop at the Old Station in Barrhead on our way home from the "pictures", I never heard him utter a swear word. Indeed when an opponent swore at him during a game, Tommy would smile, wag his finger at him and say: "You'll go to the big, bad fire."

Tommy McInally had been my idol as a boy. He was a gifted fellow human being I respected. He was simply a nice person, and marvellous company. Some of his antics weren't always appreciated. He was moved to centre-forward in the 1927 Scottish Cup final against East Fife, when Jimmy McGrory had to pull out with injury. Tommy, who had played for so long as the midfield schemer, had lost his sharpness and goal touch, and when Celtic were leading 3-1 he started play-acting by shooting from long range, and then laughing at the easy chances he muffed. Maley wasn't amused. But as McInally said later: "I'm well past being another Jimmy McGrory."

Celtic players, however, weren't all as friendly as Tommy McInally, Peter Wilson or the gentleman himself, Jimmy McGrory. Little Patsy

Gallacher was a different kettle of fish. He was a long-established Celtic player years before I ever kicked a ball for Rangers. Jimmy McGrory and Sir Robert Kelly, the late Celtic chairman, thought he was the greatest player they had ever seen. I can understand this because of the great service he gave to Celtic in his 431 games for the club over 15 years.

I thought he was a marvellous little player. No one could dribble with the ball as he could. His control was quite uncanny at times. He could change speed and direction without losing his superb balance, and his authority on the field was always obvious. If he played then Celtic played. And he could score good goals. McGrory reckoned he was the fastest player he ever saw over ten yards. This made him dangerous near the box. I chuckled when people called him a seven-stone weakling. Though he had spindly legs, and looked a bit narrow-shouldered, he had a strong body, as opponents found out. He was much tougher than he looked.

He was as good as Alex James, Andy Cunningham, Wilf Mannion, Billy Steel, Kevin Keegan, Kenny Dalglish and all the other great inside-forwards of my life. And maybe better than most. But he was a dirty wee blighter, as I found out very early in my career.

I was with Airdrie at the time, when I came face to face with Patsy playing for Celtic at Parkhead. During the game I took possession of the ball and immediately Gallacher came to tackle me. Accidentally the ball struck the toe of my boot and went between his legs. Nowadays players call it a "nutmeg". Of course he found great difficulty in turning, and I ran round him and got away. Nothing came of the move, but when I turned to run up field I was met by a furious Gallacher. He said: "You're too young to come that with me!" I attemped to explain that it had been an accident and tried to apologise. He would have none of it. Moments later as he ran past me he punched me three times right on the naughty parts, and down I went gasping. I couldn't believe it. On came the trainer, and when the referee, Tom Dougray, came over I complained bitterly about Gallacher's actions. Said Dougray: "My advice to you, son, is to stay away from him. He's too old-fashioned for you." How about that for sympathy!

Gallacher, of course, was a god as far as the Celtic fans were concerned, and why not? He helped them to win seven championships and four Scottish Cup medals, and if he'd been a Scot then he'd have won a barrowload of caps. As an Irishman he had to content himself with two or three League caps, though he was capped a dozen times for Ireland.

In my early days with Rangers it soon became apparent that there was no love lost between Gallacher and the Ibrox left-half Tully Craig, who had joined Rangers from Celtic in 1923. I almost felt sorry for Patsy during his days as a Falkirk player (he played 15 years for Celtic, then another six for Falkirk) when Tully repeatedly whacked him hard when they competed for the ball. Eventually I shouted to Tully: "Hey, aren't you overdoing it it a bit?" Replied Tully: "I'm only doing it to him before he does it to me!"

It was Gallacher of course who scored one of the most memorable Cup final goals of all time in 1925 against Dundee at Hampden. Celtic were a goal down when Patsy went off on a typical dribbling burst which took him right to the edge of the Dundee goal-line. Sheer weight of numbers stopped him, but as he fell, he gripped the ball between his feet and somersaulted into the net with the ball. The goal had the mark of a quick-thinking genius. Some minutes later Jimmy McGrory scored the winner.

I had trouble with another Celtic player, right-back Billy Cook who didn't do my health any good in the final of the Glasgow Charity Cup at Hampden in May of 1930. He knocked me unconscious! I had thrown myself at a cross ball late in the first half and made a good connection with my head. But Cook hit me with his head, and I didn't remember another thing until I opened my eyes to see my father and Bill Struth gazing down anxiously at me in the dressing-room.

Had it been bad judgment on Cook's part or had he hit me deliberately? I wondered. Anyway Cook, who had cut his head, had carried on playing. I resumed, gey shakily, five minutes after the restart. My father had been so anxious when he saw me go down, that he had run round to the front door at Hampden and demanded to be let in. The doorman tried to stop him, but failed. He looked mightily relieved when I opened my eyes, but he wasn't all that pleased when I insisted on going back on to the field.

It was a vital match for Rangers. If we won it then we'd set a world record of winning every competition we had entered that season. Rangers had already won the championship, the Scottish Cup, the Glasgow Cup and all the reserve trophies. The game ended 2-2, was still a draw after extra time, with both teams managing four corner kicks each. It was a toss-up. The Celtic skipper Jimmy McStay called wrongly, and Rangers were awarded the Cup. Two hours later we were on to the train to Greenock en route to a 14-match tour of Canada and America.

The last thing I needed was a sea voyage. My head was pounding. Now, I'm not a vindictive man but I have to admit I was determined to get back at Cook the following season. And I did. I waited until we were going into the tackle, and I deliberately went in late. Cook went down holding his ankle, and was carted off for treatment. After the game the Celtic manager Willie Maley sought me out and said: "Bob, I'm surprised at you." I said to Maley: "I was surprised at Cook in the Charity Cup final," and walked away.

Joe Kennaway who had replaced John Thomson in the Celtic goal was never too happy at playing against Rangers. He was a good 'keeper, signed by Celtic from Fall River where we had got Bob McAulay. He had been capped by America and Canada and was good enough to win two Scotland caps in 1934. Big Jimmy Smith, our centre-forward, used to tease the life out of him during the "Old Firm" games. Every time we got a corner, Smithie would shout to me: "Right, Bob, you get the ball and I'll get the goalie." Poor Joe would be trying to keep one eye on Smithie and one eye on the ball. There was one occasion when Smithie did "get the goalie" and sent Kennaway crashing into the back of the net with a tremendous shoulder charge. Nowadays Smithie would have been suspended out of sight. In these days . . . well, it was very much a man's game.

Though there was great rivalry between the two big Glasgow clubs, just as there is today, there was no real enmity. I think the proof of this was on international occasions when the Celtic and Rangers players would seek each other out to sit and talk about the game. We had so much in common, because as "Old Firm" players we had a high profile, and were always expected to win. I know that I always sought out Jimmy McGrory on these international occasions because I enjoyed playing with him so much.

I've never forgotten a brief conversation I had with Willie Maley before one of the 39 Rangers-Celtic matches I played in. I had strolled on to Celtic Park prior to the match when Maley came down the tunnel, walked up to me and said: "What takes you out here?" So I explained that I wanted to see the condition of the ground so that I'd make up my mind what kind of studs I'd use on my boots. We got round to talking about how hard the "Old Firm" matches could be and I said to him: "You know, Mr Maley, if I was playing for Celtic I'd play as hard for you as I do for Rangers." He looked at me and said: "I believe you."

Maley was my manager on one occasion only. I played in a Celtic-Rangers Select against a Hearts-Hibs Select at Tynecastle in aid of a fishing disaster, and wore a Celtic strip. I remember thinking to myself how spotlessly clean the jersey was. I was also impressed by Maley in the dressing-room. He was meticulous in everything he did and showed that he really cared about players. Just like Bill Struth.

11

Why My Parkhead Goal Gave Struth a Smile

One of the most spectacular goals I ever scored was at Celtic Park in November 1931. No it wasn't an "Old Firm" match, it was against the English Football League in the annual confrontation between the two leagues. It was a goal that had the Rangers manager Bill Struth smiling broadly — but for all the wrong reasons. I had just proved him right and in the process proved myself wrong!

Earlier in the season Struth had pulled me aside after a certain match and said to me: "Bob, if you had been upfield when that cross came over from Alan Morton you could have scored." I tried to count ten before answering him, but failed by several numbers. I had been told by Struth some time earlier that he wanted me back in our penalty area to help out our defence every time the opposition got a corner kick. The reason for this was fairly simple. Our left-half, George Brown, was almost three inches smaller than me, didn't have the physique and wasn't all that clever with his head. So I would get into the penalty area along with our defenders and "Brownie" would stay near the 18 yards line to pick up anything coming out of the defence, keep possession or make a pass that would ease the pressure on our areas.

Now here was Struth criticising me for not being up with play after I had headed clear at a corner kick in our box. I told him: "You expect me to head away corner kicks at one end and then run down field and score at the other end. That's impossible. I just can't be expected to be in two places at one time."

Struth never did like a face-to-face discussion outside his room. He looked at me, made a movement with his hands, and said: "Go on, be off with you."

So guess what happened against the English? There I was back in the Scottish penalty area as the English took a corner kick, with my

Ibrox team-mate George Brown standing somewhere outside the box. When the corner kick came over, I got to it first with my head and sent it out towards the bye-line. Wee Alan Morton got possession immediately, and took off down the left wing. He took the Leeds right-half Willis Edwards and then the Huddersfield right-back Roy Goodall, with a typical burst of ball control, on the run, and then slung the ball over into the English box. And who was there to meet it with his head and score? Right. McPhail.

I had just proved that Bill Struth did know what he was talking about, and knew exactly what I was capable of doing. As a former professional runner, he knew I had the pace to travel some 80 yards from one penalty area to the other and get myself into a scoring position.

I made sure I avoided him after the game and he made no reference to the goal that I had scored that particular day. I had proved his point.

It turned out a pretty good day for the Scots, because we beat the English 4-3 before a crowd of 51,000 in a really marvellous game of football. They had fielded their strongest team, with Harry Hibbs of Birmingham in goal, the regular England full-backs Roy Goodall of Huddersfield and Ernie Blenkinsop of Sheffield Wednesday, Sammy Crooks of Derby and Cliff Bastin of Arsenal on the wings, and Dixie Dean at centre-forward. And they started well with a goal in just five minutes from Joe Smith of Portsmouth. But we had a pretty good side ourselves, and by half-time we were leading 3-2.

Jimmy McGrory got our first goal from one of my passes. The second goal came indirectly through Jimmy, when he was sent hurtling on his face in the penalty area by the rough-and-tumble Roy Goodall. "Peter" McGonagle sank the penalty kick in the 40th minute and three minutes later I proved the Rangers manager right with that McPhail-Morton-McPhail goal which shattered the English and damned near shattered me!

A minute later Cliff Bastin got one back for England, and the Arsenal winger then got the equaliser five minutes after the interval from a nifty Dean pass. Our winner came from my good friend Jimmy McGrory in the 63rd minute. It was a Celtic goal, as Bertie Thomson, playing on the right wing, made the pass that gave Jimmy his chance.

I thought we had all played pretty well that day, though most of the praise was given to McGrory, Morton, Davie Meiklejohn, who had been at right-half, and myself.

It was during this game that wee Alan Morton had got more than a bit upset at the treatment I was getting from Goodall, a very experienced and hard full-back who was to play 25 times for England in full internationals. Wee Alan shouted: "Get the ball to me, Bob, and I'll give this big fellow something to think about." "Pinkie" made a real fool of him. So much so I began to feel sorry for Goodall. Alan Morton turned on all his tricks, beating him outside, inside and even through his legs. Goodall eventually shouted at him: "Come anywhere near me, and I'm going to kick you into the stand." It didn't put my wee partner off one little bit. After he had left him struggling with another bit of magic, Alan turned and said to Goodall: "Hey, tell me, where dae ye bury yer deid!" I couldn't help laughing, thinking: "What a cheeky wee devil!"

It must have been sheer coincidence but when England played Scotland at Wembley the following April the England right-back was Shaw of West Bromwich Albion, the only time he was ever capped. Goodall was rested! Scotland's outside-left was Morton, establishing his record 11th cap against the "Auld Enemy".

I've always felt it's a great shame that this annual representative match between the leagues of England and Scotland have long since been abandoned. I think they would be a tremendous advantage to Andy Roxburgh, our national coach, or indeed any other Scotland international manager. I thought these were ideal matches to blood future international players, and to try out formations or combinations of players.

In my day I found them much harder to play in than full internationals. In the international games you felt they were more of a show game and that you should be on your best behaviour and perhaps be more restrained, though we were, of course, trying to win. In the league games it seemed that everyone wanted to get their sleeves up and have a right good go at each other. I have no doubts that in my day many players earned their first full Scotland cap after showing up well against the English League. It was certainly the case as far as I was concerned. As an Airdrie player I played against the Irish League at Tynecastle and then the English League at Leicester before getting my first Scotland cap at Hampden Park. I think this is a much more realistic fixture than "B" internationals and it wouldn't make all that much difference to the fixture list, considering it is one extra international fixture which could be played in midweek.

I played five times against the English League and once against the Irish League — and I enjoyed them all thoroughly. It was on 27 October 1926, just two days after my 21st birthday, that I made my first

It's posing time after we've beaten St Mirren 5-0 in the 1934 Scottish Cup final, with skipper Davie Meiklejohn, in the middle, joining goal-scorers Bobby Main, Willie Nicholson (2), Jimmy Smith and myself on the track at Hampden Park.

appearance for the League against the Irishmen at Tyncastle Park. We won 5-2 mainly because our inside-forward trio of John White of Hearts, Jimmy McGrory of Celtic and myself were all big, strong players who were not afraid of a tackle.

We had the game all wrapped up in about 14 minutes. I scored in seven minutes when I knocked in a rebound from Differn, the Belfast Celtic 'keeper. McGrory left-footed a good cross from Billy Cook of Dundee into the net in 11 minutes and then John White tucked away a cross from the Celtic outside-right Pat Connolly. I got a fourth goal just before the interval, when I managed to get one on target from about 20 yards. White did even better in the 75th minute with a tremendous left-foot shot from 25 yards.

It was, of course, the first time I had played in front of the Rangers left-half of that time, Tully Craig. Here was a player's player. A grafter. A man who would fight for you and the team as long as he had breath. From the first time I played with Tully I never changed my opinion of him. He was the best.

Just five months later I found myself picked to play against the English League at Filbert Street, the ground of Leicester City. I had Tully Craig at my back again and for the first time I was to partner the man who was to become known as the "wee blue devil", Alan Morton of Rangers. My Airdrie team-mate Jackie McDougall was at centre-half. We got a 2-2 draw and Jimmy McGrory and I scored the Scottish goals.

I got the only goal in the first half, when a long ball from the Hibs right-winger Harry Ritchie was pushed through to me by Morton and I beat the Sheffield Wednesday 'keeper Joe Brown with a good right-foot shot in 12 minutes. Willie Walker, the Aston Villa inside-forward, got the equaliser and then we went behind when the 'Spurs centre-half Elkes headed a good cross from his right-winger, Urwin of Newcastle, past Tommy Ferguson, our 'keeper from Falkirk. There weren't many games in which Jimmy McGrory didn't score and this was no exception. He got the equaliser when he took a good pass from George Stevenson and easily beat the English 'keeper.

Because we had impressed the watching selectors, Bobby Thomson, the Falkirk left-back, and I got our first full caps against England at Hampden the following month. If there had been no inter-league matches how would Thomson and I have proved ourselves worthy of a full cap? There were no under-21 games nor indeed under-23 games in those days. So the value of these league matches was obvious, and at the risk of repeating myself, I think there is still a place in our fixture card for them.

After this match I had a happy reunion with my old Airdrie manager, Willie Orr. He had left Broomfield a couple of years earlier to become manager of Leicester and he was doing well. Leicester had won the Second Division championship in 1925 and were First Division runners-up in 1929. The influence of Orr, who had been a great help and adviser to me at Airdrie, was obvious. He spent most of the time trying to talk me into signing for Leicester, but when I told him Everton and Rangers were now sitting on my doorstep he just smiled and wished me the best of luck.

We didn't have too much trouble in beating the English League 3-0 at Maine Road, Manchester, in November 1932, when my left-wing

Hamilton's 'keeper Jimmy Morgan punches the ball away from Bobby Main's head during the 1935 Scottish Cup final, which we won 2-1. On the left is Jimmy McStay, and doing a bit of spectating on the right is Accies' right-half Jackie Cox and the Rangers' skipper — me.

partner was Charlie Napier of Celtic who scored two of the goals. Charlie indeed scored after just four minutes following some smart play from my Rangers team-mates Davie Meiklejohn and Sandy Archibald on the right. Then in the 67th minute Charlie showed us all what he could do with a free-kick, when his shot from some 25 yards completely shattered Harry Hibbs in the English goal. Neilly Dewar, the Third Lanark centre-forward, got our third goal from a pass from another of my Rangers team-mates, Doc Marshall, 15 minutes from the end. We had played well and personally I felt I had played my best representative match to date, even though I hadn't managed to get on the scoring list.

This was the first time I had played with Charlie Napier and though it would be wrong of me to compare him with Alan Morton, I did enjoy playing with him. He was a great player to have in your side, because he always wanted to be involved. He played hard and worked hard and wouldn't hesitate to move to the other side of the field to get at the ball. Earlier that year he had played against England at Wembley at inside-left to Alan Morton as I was "indisposed". And in 1935 he played at outside-right for Scotland against England at Hampden in a 2-0 win. So Charlie was quite a versatile chap and went on to give service to Derby County when he left Celtic. He was certainly my kind of player.

I skippered the 1934 League side against the English at Ibrox where we had Celtic's Canadian-born Joe Kennaway in goal, Bobby Main and Willie Nicholson of Rangers on the wings, and Andy Anderson of Hearts and the incomparable "Peter" McGonagle of Celtic at full-back. In passing I should point out that Kennaway was the first foreign player to win a Scottish Cup medal, with Celtic in 1933 and again in 1937.

Now, I thought our "Whitey" McDonald at Ibrox could throw a ball until I saw Stan Weaver of Newcastle United, who was at inside-left for the English side that day. "Whitey's" throws were high and long. Weaver's came into the penalty area like a cannon ball. I've never seen a player throw a ball with such power since. Weaver was a very strong man. I had played against him in the full international at Hampden the previous year, when we won 2-1. Weaver was then at left-half and fortunately his reputation as a long-throw expert was well known to us. Even so, he was always a danger when the ball was in his hands.

One vivid memory I have of the '34 League game is big Jimmy Simpson, the Rangers centre-half, doing a fair imitation of a tribal war dance in the middle of the field, after scoring with a free-kick after about 11 minutes. When his shot beat Ted Sagar of Everton he threw his hands in the air and looked as though he was going to jump into the enclosure. I burst out laughing. I couldn't help it.

Jimmy, whose son Ronnie was the Celtic 'keeper in that memorable European Cup win in Lisbon in 1967, was very much the stopper centre-half. He stopped people very well indeed, in the air and on the ground, but wasn't the cleverest player with the ball at his feet. Indeed I recall Alex Venters once saying to me: "Hey, Bob I got a pass from big Jimmy today. But I had to go up into the stand to collect it!" Said in jest,

Helping my lovely wife Jessie to cut the cake at our wedding reception in 1933 in Glasgow's Marlborough House. My best man is brother-in-law John Richmond, the bridesmaid is Jessie's cousin, Nan Braidwood. I remember it well. It was the year we regained the League Championship from Motherwell.

of course, as part of the great rivalry which exists between defenders and forwards. So Jimmy's spectacular goal, which he certainly enjoyed, put us in front. But not for long. Beresford hit a good equaliser just two minutes later and we knew we were in for a hard game.

Bowers of Derby County then put the English ahead, but I got the equaliser with a goal that gave me a lot of satisfaction. I took a throw-in from George Brown, turned quickly, and hit the ball as hard as I could with my right foot. The shot was a low one but Sagar, who became a legend in the Everton side, somehow got across the goal. Though he got his fingers to it he couldn't stop it and he only managed to divert the ball into the net. I felt the 60,000 crowd — and Ibrox can't accommodate that amount of people nowadays — had been given good value for money.

My final game against the English League at Everton's Goodison

120

Park in 1936 was not a memorable occasion. We lost 2-0. Cliff Bastin scored from the penalty spot after Tom Smith, our centre-half from Kilmarnock, had fouled Ray Westwood of Bolton in the box, and then Westwood scored the second goal from a slick through pass from Dixie Dean. Both goals were scored in the first half and we just couldn't fight our way back.

Our left-back was a young fellow from Airdrie named Jock Shaw, who was to join Rangers two years later and earn the nickname "Tiger" as captain of the club. Most of the talk before that match centred round the Scottish inside-right Tommy Walker, now an automatic choice in the Scotland international team. The rumours were that he was being transferred to Arsenal for £12,000. It didn't happen. Hearts said the offer was poor and Tommy stayed at Tynecastle.

Our wingers in that game were Jimmy Delaney of Celtic and Davie Kinnear, a Fifer from Kirkcaldy who had joined Rangers two years earlier, and Matt Armstrong from Aberdeen was at centre-forward. The 25,000 crowd saw some excellent football from the Arsenal right-back George Male, Everton's right-half Cliff Britton, right-winger Sammy Crooks of Derby County and, of course, Cliff Bastin the exciting Arsenal left-winger. But they had to be impressed by our 'keeper, Jerry Dawson of Rangers. He was now firmly established as Scotland's No. 1 'keeper and he proved it on this particular visit to Liverpool.

A number of players I played alongside in these league matches never ever won a full cap. Men like Jimmy McStay, an outstanding centre-half with Celtic, who is a great uncle of Paul McStay, now established at Parkhead, and his team-mate Chic Geatons, Falkirk 'keeper Tommy Ferguson, our own outside-left Willie Nicholson, Hearts right-back Reid, and Dundee centre-half Rankine. Their reward for sheer consistency of performance during a season was to play for the Scottish League. Unfortunately they were never given any tangible reward, as the League secretary of that time, Willie McAndrew, wasn't one to throw money about.

The dark blue shirt you wore with pride in these games had to be handed back. You did not get a memento of the occasion, and if my memory serves me right you got a match fee of about £6. Now I had played before 51,000 at Celtic Park and 60,000 at Ibrox for the Scottish League. Surely from the money they got from these games and the share of the games played in England they could at least have let the players keep their jerseys. These were definitely the dark ages as far as

Skipper Davie Meiklejohn joins the goal-scorers, me, Sam English and Jimmy Fleming after our 3-0 Scottish Cup win over Kilmarnock in 1932 when our heavy coats had the distinctive look of a job lot.

financial philanthropy in football was concerned!

Some of the greatest names in Scottish football history cut their international teeth in these league games. Players like Third Lanark 'keeper Jimmy Brownlie, who played 14 times for the League, Alex "The Icicle" McNair, the Celtic right-back (14), Jimmy McMenemy of Celtic, who like myself won seven Scottish Cup medals (13), Alex Smith, the great Rangers outside-left (14), and that superb Hearts inside-right Bobby Walker (12). The "wee blue devil" himself, Alan Morton, was always proud to say that he had played 12 times in various games for the Scottish League. They were the next best to playing in a full international.

With the removal of these inter-league games I feel that the administrators of the game in Scotland, and indeed in England, paid scant regard to their historical significance, and indeed seemed quite sacrilegious in their haste to dump them. Old fashioned? I don't think so!

12

When Bill Shankly and I were Saints

My days were numbered as a Rangers player at the start of season 1939-40, which had no chance of being completed because of a mad housepainter called Adolf Hitler. Chamberlain's "peace in our time" became a bloody conflict in Europe and after five games the league championship was over. There would be no full-time football as long as there was war.

Suddenly we were all part-time players looking for a job, with players throughout the country being allowed a maximum payment of £2 a week. As the clubs lost players to the forces, the shipyards, munitions, forestry and other war effort callings, it was decided that football would continue, in regional leagues.

The British public would need distractions, entertainment and sport to help see them through the dark uncertain days of attrition and its despairs. Clubs were therefore able to use players from anywhere to fill their ranks on a Saturday afternoon. This was freedom of contract with a vengeance. Contracts were torn up as part of the war effort, as players who became servicemen began playing with the clubs nearest to their training camps.

At the age of 34 I was too old for call-up and began working at Weir's of Cathcart, helping to assemble heavy artillery guns for the army. Rangers became part of the Scottish Southern League, and though I had lost my first-team place to Alex Venters, I was called upon to make five more appearances for Rangers in the new war-time league, and scored two goals.

At the end of the season I was given a free transfer. It was simply time to go. As far as I was concerned my career was over. I decided there and then to hang up my boots. I wouldn't play again.

My brother Malcolm, a former Kilmarnock winger who had a

successful bakery business in Barrhead, was now a director of St Mirren. He had other thoughts. He asked me to play for St Mirren because he thought my experience and my influence would help the young players they had at Love Street. At first I resisted his persistent overtures, but eventually I agreed that I would play once I had got myself back to a reasonable state of fitness.

So on the first Saturday in January of 1941, I made my debut for the Saints at inside-right. It was a strange feeling, after wearing the light blue of Rangers for so long. We were playing Hearts at Paisley. And making his one and only appearance ever for St Mirren at right-half behind me was Bill Shankly of Preston North End. The St Mirren team was: Johnstone; Savage and Craven; Shankly, McDowall, Urquhart; Caskie, McPhail, Linwood, Stead and Deakin.

I think Shankly, who was then established as Scotland's right-half, was a PT instructor with the RAF at Bishopbriggs, near Glasgow. He was a good, hard player who always seemed to be on the tips of his toes as he chased and harried all over the place. A great worker. Little did I think then, though, that his greatest days would be as the creator of the superb modern Liverpool side, which he built back in 1958, instilling a system of play which is even being used today with such devastating effect.

The combination of Shankly and McPhail, however, didn't quite work out. We lost 1-0. Mind, it didn't help when we lost our 'keeper Bobby Johnstone with a broken leg just after the start of the second-half and had to play with ten men. It meant that Shankly finished up at right-back, Joe Craven, later to join Rangers and become their assistant trainer, went into goal, and I was pulled back to half-back.

I had changed clubs, with reluctance, but I was still a greetin'-faced big B! My wee right-winger was Jimmy Caskie who was to win eight wartime caps, and eventually played for Rangers. Well, I gave him a real mouthful during the game because of his tanner ba' tactics out on the wing. Instead of whipping the ball across quickly with his right foot, he would show how clever he was and beat the full-back two or three times before crossing with his left foot. After being caught three or four times offside I lost my patience. So I bellowed: "Are you playing for St Mirren, or are you playing for yourself? Will you get that bloody ball over quickly and stop fan-dancing about!" He didn't like it. But my new team-mates did. One shouted over: "Well said, Bob. Someone's been needing to tell him that for a long time."

Maybe it was coincidence but in my next game for St Mirren against

*Celtic 'keeper John Thomson foils Jimmy Fleming during the 1928 Scottish Cup
final, watched anxiously by Tommy McInally, "Jean" McFarlane and Peter Wilson.*

Falkirk at Love Street, Caskie had been switched to outside-left!
Falkirk beat us 4-3 with the winning goal coming from a former Celtic
opponent of mine, Charlie "happy feet" Napier who was playing at left-
half, as my direct opponent. Also in the Falkirk side was my former
Rangers team-mate Jimmy Fiddes who had played in the Scottish
Cup-winning side against Third Lanark. Jimmy was then an outside-
right. For Falkirk he was at right-half and I thought he played rather
well.

I recall playing with Jimmy in a Rangers side against Falkirk and scoring a goal I was rather proud of. The ball had been lobbed forward, and I had hit it on the drop from the edge of the penalty area and sent it with considerable venom into the back of the net. Fiddes, then a young player, looked at me and said: "Oh my, that was some goal. Did you pick your spot?" With a straight face I replied: "Aye, I just picked out a wee square of the netting and hit the ball with it." It took him two or three seconds to realise I was taking the mickey.

Though I had been in the losing side in my first two games for the Saints, I quickly realised they had a number of good players, and they would fight hard for each other. I had scored my first goal for Saints in the game with Falkirk, so I felt I was beginning to settle in with my new team-mates.

Like all clubs they had their characters. The one I remember most was the right-half Willie Kelly. Now, after every home game at Love Street, we would come out of the dressing-room, and form a queue going upstairs leading to the manager's office. Sammy Blythe was a nice wee man, with a bit of a stutter, and as he was the manager it was his job to hand out the required £2 to each of the players. We would walk into his room, one after the other in quick succession and lift the £2 being counted out by Sammy, who had a habit of not looking up at the player taking the money. Willie Kelly twigged this and no sooner had he lifted his two quid than he dashed back to the end of the queue, and picked up another two quid! Sammy never could work out how he kept being two pounds short.

In my third game St Mirren played really well to give Hibs their first home defeat of the season at Easter Road. We beat them 4-2. I scored the second goal and our centre-forward Alex Linwood, who was one of the best I had seen in years, scored twice. By this time I was operating at inside-left to the exclusion of a very good young player in Angus Stead, with Johnny Deakin as my left-wing partner.

Just after this match Sammy Blythe resigned. There was immediate speculation that Bobby Ferrier or George Stevenson of the great Motherwell side, or myself, would be offered the job. I wasn't approached directly, but I made it clear I was not at all interested. The new manager turned out to be former Cowdenbeath centre-half Donald Menzies who had played alongside George Brown, my ex-Ibrox team-mate and Davie Hope, the late Rangers director who founded Ibrox Pools, with Ashfield Juniors in Glasgow.

In all I played 13 games for St Mirren and scored seven goals. I had the great pleasure of helping the Saints to beat Celtic 1-0 at Love

Rangers skipper Davie Meiklejohn, the most influential player at Ibrox during my career, leads 'keeper Tom Hamilton and the rest of the Ibrox players on to Hampden for yet another Scottish Cup final.

Street where Alex Linwood was the match-winner. I also recall a hectic 5-5 draw with Hamilton Accies at Douglas Park where their centre-forward Davie Wilson, a really good player, scored a hat-trick and I managed one.

Maybe my most satisfying game was at Coatbridge where I scored both the Saints goals in a 2-1 win over Albion Rovers. I remember this as a really hard game. My winner came when the Rovers defence tried to play me offside and failed. I held on to the ball as the defenders screamed at the referee and took my time in beating their 'keeper.

My last game in a St Mirren strip was against Rangers. It was the semi-final of the wartime Scottish Cup at Hampden Park and there was a crowd of 36,823 to see it. It was a very funny feeling to play against a club that had been so much of my life for so long. While with Airdrie I had twice scored the winning goal against Rangers and indeed had never played in a losing side against them. Could I keep my record going? The Rangers side was: Dawson; Gray, Shaw; Bolt, Woodburn, Symon; Waddell, Thornton, Smith, Venters, Johnstone.

I had the chance to score early in the game but I funked it. Newspaper reports suggested that I seemed a bit slow in going for the chance. The truth was that I felt if I had scored then I would have had my leg broken! The Rangers centre-half, Willie Woodburn, was coming in fast to make his tackle and looked to me like being a fraction late. Having played with Woodburn in my last season at Ibrox I knew there was no way he would pull back. So I chickened out. I threw the scoring chance away by deliberately hesitating.

Woodburn knew what had gone on in my mind. He looked at me and said: "I wouldn't have hurt you, Bob." I said: "Willie, knowing you, you'd probably have killed me." Woodburn turned out to be one of the best centre-halfs Rangers ever had, but he could be ruthless. He was never one to take prisoners.

Rangers won 4-1 with their goals coming from wee Charlie Johnstone, Willie Thornton, Willie Waddell, with a tremendous left-footer, and Jimmy Smith. Jimmy Caskie scored for St Mirren, and it was a real cracker. He hit the ball from the edge of the box, giving Jerry Dawson no chance. Jimmy, I thought, was our best forward and it didn't really surprise me that he was in Scotland's first wartime international against England at Hampden the following month.

It turned out to be another good season for Rangers. They won that wartime Cup, beating Hearts 4-2 in the final after a 1-1 draw, and they won the newly formed 16-club league championship by three points from Clyde. St Mirren finished seventh. Rangers also won the Glasgow Charity Cup by beating Partick Thistle 3-0 in the final, when their outside-right was the one and only Stan Matthews, who was now in the RAF. Matthews in a Rangers strip! Who said the English invasion started when Graeme Souness became the Ibrox manager?

There was still the Summer Cup to be played for, but it wasn't for me. It had been agreed that I would play for the Saints only until the league finished in May. Though I did play two more games for my old pal Tully Craig, whom I enjoyed having at my back on so many occasions as a Rangers player.

Tully was now manager of Falkirk, and was keen to win the Stirlingshire Cup. He asked me to help him out. I did. I played two games and thoroughly enjoyed them. Unfortunately Tully didn't win his Stirlingshire Cup.

You just know when it is time to stop playing. My days were over. It was time to look to a future away from football. But first of all I had to get on with the job of constructing heavy artillery for the Army and, even if I say so myself, became extremely proficient at what I was doing. To such an extent that when the war finished I was offered a job in the planing machine section of the Dubbs engineering firm in the south side of Glasgow.

It didn't take me long to realise that the confines of factory work in peace-time was making me one very unhappy man. So when I was offered a job as a salesman by a Glasgow electrical equipment supplier called Willie Harper, I jumped at it. Particularly as a car went with the job. It helped that Willie was a rabid Rangers fan.

I learned my trade as a salesman the hard way, and found myself enjoying discovering the mysteries of valves, condensers and plugs. It was a customer of mine, Peter Gordon, another Rangers fan, who suggested I should have my own place. It was now 1948.

With some financial help from my next-door neighbour, Gordon Meikle, I took over premises in Glasgow's West Campbell Street, and that's how my company, McPhail and Meikle Ltd, was formed, and 40 years later is still going strong, with me as managing director.

Some 18 months later I bought out Gordon in amicable circumstances, and my wife Jessie became my book-keeper overnight, working out the invoices and the advice notes until the wee sma' hours.

Nowadays my son Robbie, an accountant, who played rugby all his life, and my grand-nephew John, who is also an accountant, run the business, with me very much in the background, as the oldest message boy in town.

Changed days indeed from my days during the war when I would travel to Weir's of Cathcart from Giffnock each day by bicycle, with my wife giving the daily warning to be careful when returning late in the black-out, particularly if we were having a visit from German bombers.

I remember returning from a night-shift at 8 a.m. and, being the considerate type, I entered my home quietly, and took a peep into the bedroom. There was no one there!

The bed hadn't been slept in. Somewhat alarmed I made a search of the house, but couldn't find my wife.

Returning to the bedroom I noticed a slight movement of the curtain near the bed. When I went over, there, fast asleep and tucked *under* the bed, was Jessie, looking quite comfy. She had read somewhere that the safest place in a house during an air-raid was under the bed, as the springs of a mattress would help resist falling debris.

There had been an air-raid that night, and Jessie was one who believed everything she read in a newspaper. I fairly embellished that story over the years.

13

These Ibrox "Masters" Would Still be No. 1

I would argue, as long as it takes, that the greatest Rangers team from any period in the long and quite illustrious history of the club would come from my time at Ibrox in the "Throbbing Thirties", when thousands had to be turned away from games. I have seen all the great Rangers squads from 1920 to the present day from close quarters, as I have been directly involved with the club for the past 60 years. So I feel my assessment should not be considered biased by those who watch the modern game.

I've known since the day I kicked my first ball for Rangers back in 1927 that it takes a special kind of footballer to establish himself at Ibrox, as indeed it does at Parkhead. Even though I had won a Scottish Cup medal with Airdrie and had been capped against England while at Broomfield, there was no guarantee that I would fit into the Ibrox set-up. I had to work at it.

Nothing has changed over the years. It is not just good enough to play well. You've got to be a winner. You've got to be consistent week in and week out, hail, rain or sunshine, month after month, season after season. You've got to learn to take stick from the crowd and from your opponents, who will always try and raise their game because it's Rangers they are playing. There is no respite if you win a cup. You've got to go out and do it again the following season.

As a Rangers player you must convince yourself that you are better than your opponent, and then you've got to prove it. You must have confidence in your own ability, display a little arrogance, and if the going gets tough then you've got to stand up and be counted. It's still a man's game. There is no hiding place for a player at Ibrox. You are public property and every game is a cup final. You play before big crowds every week, and they expect nothing but the best.

Celtic have the same attitude. They had it in my day, and justifiably so, as they were always our greatest rivals in cup and league football.

Aberdeen won all the domestic trophies and the European Cup Winners Cup because their players developed confidence in their own skilful abilities under Alex Ferguson, with international players like Gordon Strachan, Willie Miller, Alex McLeish, Jim Leighton and Eric Black. And wasn't it the sheer consistency of performance from players like Dave Narey, Hamish McAlpine, Paul Hegarty, Paul Sturrock, Richard Gough and Davie Dodds under Jim McLean, that pushed Dundee United to the forefront of Europe and at home?

At Ibrox, however, second best is unacceptable and the good players have to learn to live with this. I've seen them come and go at Ibrox for the past 60 years and you soon learn to pick out the ones who are going to make it and those who would be better with clubs that are not expected to win anything.

Pressure? I never felt any when I was a player. I don't think any of us did. Under Bill Struth we just went into every match expecting to win it. And, if we didn't, the dressing-room inquest was indescribable, without Struth having to say a word! It was really all about the pride in being a Rangers player.

Looking back at the great names I played alongside in those glory days of the late 1920s and the 1930s I am now more convinced than ever that the players from that period would have beaten any club side in the world. Aye, even today.

Now this is no criticism of the modern players by an old pro, who has blinkered memories of the "good old days". It is an honest assessment of all the teams which have helped give Rangers their worldwide appeal, and in a sense is a tribute to the men of my generation.

Ever since I hung up my boots some 46 years ago, I have been asked by many people to make comparisons between the past and present players at Ibrox. Of course it makes for good meaty argument and that's what I'm offering right here. This book gives me the opportunity to go public, and name the best Rangers team from my years at Ibrox. The men I would have had by my side. Here it is:

Jerry Dawson
Dougie Gray   Bob McAulay
Jock Buchanan   Davie Meiklejohn   Tully Craig
Sandy Archibald   Andy Cunningham   Sam English   Bob McPhail   Alan Morton

Every man in that team had the qualities demanded by our manager,

The former Rangers skipper and manager John Greig would have found a place in any Ibrox squad — even the great Bill Struth side of the '30s. His indomitable spirit and competitive attitude was tremendous. He'd have been in my side, at left-back.

Bill Struth. They had an aura of success in the way they played. Every one of them would have fought for an inch of advantage on any field. Most were physically tough, but players like English and Morton had a toughness that had little to do with physique. I think they call it guts. All of them were international players, with a collective total of 118 caps, with English getting two caps with Northern Ireland.

My choice wasn't easy. I've had to leave out men like Tom Hamilton, Jimmy Simpson, George Brown, Tommy Muirhead, Jimmy Smith, Doc Marshall, Jimmy Fleming, "Whitey" MacDonald, Alex Venters and Torry Gillick, who were quite outstanding Rangers players and who contributed considerably to the rich history of the club.

The best skipper I ever played under, anywhere, was Davie Meiklejohn. His influence on Rangers was incalculable. I've never seen a better centre-half in my life-time, and I've been around for a wee bit. But "Meek" was such a complete footballer he could have played anywhere on the field. He was no taller than I, five feet ten inches, yet he could get himself up to meet those cross-balls with brilliant timing to beat players much taller than himself.

Like all the great players I've seen, he always seemed to have time and space to do the things he wanted to do with the ball. He was a brilliant passer, with both feet, and when he cleared with his head he invariably found a team-mate. When Davie played at centre-half, before the arrival of Jimmy Simpson, he would nod the ball with considerable grace to either of his half-backs or else send it further to myself or whoever was at inside-right. His timing was quite brilliant. He never looked under pressure, always seemed in control of the ball, and in the days when he would play at right-half he would come up and have a pop at goal along with the rest of us.

As a captain Meiklejohn was simply the best. His influence on the players around him, and his encouragement to younger players, was a responsibility he accepted without a worry. Struth knew he had a genius in his defence, and knew he was a lucky man to have him. "Meek", who was born within walking distance of Ibrox, played 635 games for Rangers from 1919 until his last game against Hearts at Ibrox on 22 April 1936. He played in 13 championship-winning sides, won five Scottish Cup medals, and played 15 times for Scotland, six times as captain. Rangers have never had a greater servant.

How does he compare with Terry Butcher, who skippered Rangers to their 1987 championship win? "Meek" was a better footballer. Butcher is, without doubt, a world-class defender by modern

Winning smiles from Graeme Souness and skipper Graham Roberts after beating Everton in a penalty shoot-out in Dubai in 1987 in an unofficial British Championship decider. Souness is one of the best midfield players I've ever seen in a Rangers jersey, while Davie Meiklejohn would have approved of Roberts' competitive edge!

standards and his height and weight make him invaluable in a crowded penalty area. He's also a fine ambassador for the club as he mingles easily with people, but "Meek" had the edge because of the sheer accuracy of his play.

Every great side needs a great goalkeeper and there has never been anyone better than Jerry Dawson in my opinion. He had the safest hands of any 'keeper I've seen, and he was playing in the days of the heavy leather ball, which used to gather weight during the wet, muddy winter conditions.

135

Jerry came from Falkirk. He was a highly nervous fellow. He could never keep his hands at peace. His eyes, dark brown, were always moving. He was a strong man, with big hands, and there was never any doubt about how good he was going to become when he took over from Tom Hamilton. He had superb positional sense, was nimble on his feet and always worked at being safe rather than spectacular. Mind you, he made some spectacular saves for Rangers and was known in his time as "the prince of goalkeepers". Jerry played 14 times for Scotland and in many wartime internationals. He won five championship medals and two Scottish Cup medals. But for the war there would have been many, many more honours.

Yes, he was better than Harry Hibbs, Elisha Scott, Frank Swift, Bill Merrick, Pat Jennings, Gordon Banks, Bill Brown, Peter Shilton and Alan Rough and the rest. I should add that the safest pair of hands I've seen since Jerry belong to the present Rangers 'keeper, Chris Woods. I am very impressed with this lad. I hope he stays at Ibrox until the end of his career.

My full-backs Dougie Gray, an Aberdonian, and Bob McAulay had totally different personalities. Dougie was extremely fast on his feet, quick off his mark and was a highly strung player. I just don't know how often he saved us goals by kicking a ball off the line when Jerry or Tom were beaten. He played well over 900 games for the club from 1925 to 1946, won ten championship medals, six Scottish Cup medals and was capped a mere ten times. When you talk of consistency you talk of "schnozzle", as he was known in the dressing-room.

Bob McAulay was a complete extrovert. He was signed by Bill Struth during our 1930 tour of America, when Bob was playing for Fall River. Because he had lived in America he was promptly nicknamed "Al Capone", and tried to live up to that name on the field. He would frighten the life out of his opponents with his intimidating patter. He would go into detail about what he was going to do to them on the field, which he rarely did. He had strong legs, tackled strongly and made good passes. His sharp wit was much appreciated in the dressing-room. It might have been a bit too sharp for Bill Struth, because he was transferred to Chelsea after our cup final win over Kilmarnock in 1932.

Jock Buchanan and I signed for Rangers within months of each other. Jock had been transferred from Morton for what, on the surface, seemed cover for Tommy Muirhead who had been having injury problems. But I think wee Alan Morton got it right when he said: "Jock supplied Rangers with the punch, when they needed it most." Jock was

There's no danger of Chris Woods dropping this bag. In my opinion the Rangers 'keeper has the safest pair of hands I've seen since the days of Jerry Dawson. He's been an outstanding success since he joined the club from Norwich.

Alan Morton looks quite pleased at being Rangers' captain for the day prior to an "Old Firm" match at Ibrox. The Celtic skipper is Willie McStay and the referee is Tom Small, who seems to have lost his whistle.

John Greig and Roy Aitken rolled into one. A 90-minute man who fought for every ball. Oh, he was tough all right, but he could play. It was maybe significant that when Rangers won the Scottish Cup for the first time in 25 years in 1928 the Rangers right-half was Buchanan.

I chose Tully Craig as my left-half ahead of George Brown, because this hard-working man from Lauriston was what we call in our business a "player's player". You really had to play with him to appreciate what a marvellous player he was. He was always greetin' at people. Was never off your back. He would rather hit an early pass than run with the ball, and this was his strength as far as forwards were concerned. He made it easier for us. He was a great provider for wee Alan and myself. Off the field you couldn't get a cheerier wee fellow.

This was Davie Meiklejohn's favourite photograph. Alone in the middle of Hampden Park with the Scottish Cup in 1928, to end a 25-year-old jinx. Davie's opening goal from the penalty spot, was one of the most important in the club's history.

Tully was 12 years with Rangers, won eight championship medals, two Scottish Cup medals and was capped seven times.

My right-winger, Sandy Archibald, had pace, courage and a tremendous shot. He would carry the ball to two or three yards from the bye-line then whip it over without hesitation. This was a nightmare for retreating defenders, but marvellous for running forwards to shoot or head the ball on the run. Signed from Raith Rovers, Sandy played 667 games for Rangers during his 17 years with the club and scored 162 goals. Like "Meek" he won a record 13 championship medals, played in three cup-winning sides, and made eight appearances for Scotland. He was a real tradesman.

Nobody hit the ball harder than my inside-right, Andy Cunningham. He was a natural left-footer and I recall one game where he hit the ball so hard into the net that the pegs holding the net on the ground were ripped out of the turf. I tried for years to emulate that shot, and failed miserably.

If people thought I was greetin'-faced, you should have heard Andy on the field! Because of his blond hair and fair skin he was easily conspicuous. He didn't run a lot. He didn't have to. He would stroll around the middle of the field, take the ball easily under control, and then set the attack moving with his crisp passing. He was always lying around the edge of the box ready to let fly.

I remember playing against him for the first time when I was with Airdrie. Our manager Willie Orr, a great tactician, told me to keep the ball away from Cunningham at all costs. "Even if you have to kick it back to the 'keeper or give it back to a defender, just make sure Cunningham doesn't get it. If he doesn't play then Rangers don't play." Well, I did what I was told, much to Cunningham's anger. When I nipped the ball away from him on one occasion he shouted: "You do that again and I'll slap your bloody ear." I replied: "You're not fast enough to catch me!" Was he angry!

He was never one of my closest friends at Ibrox, simply because he was 14 years older than I was. He was a great player, though, and proved it by playing until he was almost 40. He won ten championship medals, got his only cup medal in 1928, and was capped for Scotland 12 times, which was remarkable considering he got his first cap at the age of 29.

Elsewhere in this book you'll learn why I preferred Sam English as my centre-forward to Jimmy Smith or Jimmy Fleming. Maybe the fact that Sam's 44 goals in 35 league games in season 1931-32 is still a

Jerry Dawson, my favourite 'keeper, makes friends with the giant German 'keeper Hans Jacob prior to the 1936 international at Hampden Park, where Jerry had his first Scotland shut-out in a 2-0 victory.

Rangers record to this day, might be explanation enough.

No difficulty in naming the "wee blue devil" himself, Alan Morton, as my outside-left. He was simply in a class by himself. A mining engineer in Airdrie by day, a professional footballer on a Saturday afternoon, he trained only on evenings. He was less than five feet five inches in height and barely ten stones in weight. What an entertainer!

Like myself he was a natural right-footed player and would work the ball with his right foot, though he could use his left foot to good advantage. He hated heading the ball. For a wee man he had an extremely long stride and always seemed to have his body half-bent over the ball. He would never beat his opponent the same way twice.

Outside, inside or through his legs "Pinkie", as we called him, would torment the life out of full-backs. He was always shouting for the ball. "Right, Bobby, out here." "Hey, I hope you haven't forgotten me" or "It's getting cold out here." He was easy to play with. He took all his corner kicks with his right foot, to get that peculiar inswinging, hanging lob of his. It was like hitting a sand-iron as against a No. 8 iron. You could see 'keepers hesitating, as the famous Morton lob seemed to hang in the air. It got us many a goal. He wasn't particularly fast, but he was nimble of foot and thought, and was always in the right place at the right time.

A bachelor all his life, Alan played a record 11 times against England in 31 international appearances. He won nine championship medals and two Scottish Cup medals, making 495 appearances for Rangers and scoring 115 goals. He must have been 39 when he made his international farewell in Paris in 1932. The wee man was simply a magician.

Of course there were other outstanding Rangers teams. Indeed the Rangers team of the early 1920s wasn't so bad: Robb; Manderson, McCandless; Meiklejohn, Dixon and Muirhead; Archibald, Cunningham, Henderson, Cairns and Morton. Good enough to win a handful of championships.

What about the great "Iron Curtain" team of the late 1940s: Brown; Young, Shaw; McColl, Woodburn, Cox; Waddell, Duncanson, Thornton, Williamson and Rutherford? This was a hard team to beat, with big George Young providing the kind of captaincy and influence that the "Meek" had shown in my days.

I know there would be a lot of voting for the early 1960's team, inspired by the brilliant ball control of Ian McMillan and Jim Baxter. Remember it? Ritchie; Shearer and Caldow; Greig, McKinnon,

The "wee blue devil" himself, Alan Morton, as he holds off a determined Partick Thistle defender. Alan is wearing the all-white "change" shirt we wore on occasions.

Baxter; Henderson, McMillan, Miller, Brand and Wilson.

I liked the early 1970's team which won the European Cup Winners Cup in Barcelona: McCloy; Jardine, Mathieson; Greig, Johnstone, Smith; McLean, Conn, Stein, MacDonald and Johnston. A lot of good footballers in that team, I thought.

143

This Rangers squad of players was one of the finest I ever played with. In season 1929-30 it swept the boards, winning the League Championship, Scottish Cup, Glasgow Cup and Glasgow Charity Cup, losing a mere six of the 52 games we played. The names are — back row: (left to right) Trainer Jimmy Kerr, Davie Meiklejohn, Jimmy Marshall, Sandy Archibald, Jimmy Fleming, Tom Hamilton, Jock Buchanan, Tully Craig and manager Bill Struth. Front: George Brown, Dougie Gray, "Whitey" McDonald, Tommy Muirhead (captain), Bob McPhail, Bob Hamilton, Willie Nicholson and Alan Morton.

And of course there was a lot of enjoyment in watching Rangers win the 1986-87 championship with a team on these lines: Woods; Nicholl, Munro; Roberts, Butcher, Durrant; Ferguson, Souness, McCoist, Fleck and Cooper.

Of all the Rangers players I've seen since I hung up my boots in 1941, and I have seen them all, it is my opinion that only Graeme Souness, Jim Baxter, Ian McMillan, Sammy Cox and John Greig would have had any chance of breaking into *my* team.

When I see Souness play today I only wish he had been around when I was a player. I would love to have played with him. He is the perfect midfield player. He does everything right, including realeasing the ball on his first touch, which is so vital to creative play. Of course he is a hard player. You have to be playing at this level. He'd have been a big favourite with Bill Struth. That's for sure, and that's as big a compliment as I can pay Graeme.

You simply couldn't ignore the brilliance of Baxter, with that marvellous left leg of his. But I remember telling Jim many years ago while Rangers were in England playing a testimonial match for someone: "Jim, if you'd learn to release the ball quicker you'd improve your game no end." He looked at me and replied: "Ach you've got to show your opponents how real football is played, haven't you?" Jim just loved to be the entertainer, the crowd pleaser, who was the apple of Scot Symon's eye. He just played the game the way he saw it. And he did it rather well, didn't he?

Ian McMillan, like myself a product of Airdrie, had so much class in his play he could have played in any Rangers team.

John Greig? I'd have played him at left-back, where accurate passing isn't quite so vital. His physical strength, sheer stamina, and ferocious competitive spirit would have forced him into any Rangers side. Sammy Cox, who was quicker on his feet, but tackled like a tiger, had the same spirit. He was a player you would just have to use somewhere in your side.

Do I hear claims for George Young, Jock Shaw, Ian McColl, Willie Woodburn, Willie Waddell, Willie Thornton, Jimmy Millar, Ralph Brand, Willie Henderson, Davy Wilson, Davie Cooper and Ally McCoist? I certainly hope so, because they have all been outstanding Rangers players in their time. When I look at all the Rangers players of the past 60 years I really couldn't sit down and pick a super team from so many generations. It would be impossible.

But I do know that the team that I played in would have been a force in football right now. They were that good.

14

Hands Up! I was Guilty

I had a good old chuckle to myself at the furore that followed Diego Maradona's first goal against England in the World Cup quarter-final in Mexico's Azteca Stadium in 1986. The TV cameras showed clearly, time after time, that the crafty wee Argentinian skipper had punched the ball past Peter Shilton into the net. But it had obviously not been very clear to the thousands who had actually been at the game. The speed of Maradona's reactions, when he realised he was going to miss the ball with his head, had fooled them.

The whole affair brought back to me, with stunning clarity, the day I scored a goal in almost the same circumstances against Jack Harkness in the Hearts goal in 1932. I admit it now for the first time. I used my fist!

When Maradona was accused of cheating by the Press in the noisy, turbulent after-match conference he had the grace to smile and say: "I think the hand of God played a little part in that goal." How I wish I had thought of that lovely line 54 years earlier. The "hand of God" indeed! I like that.

As you will remember, Argentina beat England 2-1 in that quarter-final with Maradona scoring both goals. They then went on to beat West Germany in the final with Maradona proving to the millions who watched on TV why Naples paid £5.5 million for his transfer, and were quite happy to give him £500,000 a year. With the TV cameras around, Maradona just couldn't deny he had used his fist instead of his head to beat the unhappy Peter Shilton, who is still not convinced that the referee and linesman didn't see what happened.

Well, there were no TV cameras in my day. And though Jack Harkness shouted and roared at the top of his voice that I had used my fist to beat him, the referee would have none of it. I'll never forget the look on Jack's face after I put the ball in the net. He just couldn't believe the referee had awarded a goal. He shouted at me: "McPhail . . . McPhail . . . tell the referee you punched the ball into the net." I looked at Jack, before I ran up the field and said: "Don't be so bloody stupid!"

It was a vital goal for Rangers, because it came four minutes from the end of a League match at Ibrox, and it tied the game at 4-4! Having now come clean that I did punch the ball into the net on that occasion, I must add that if I had tried the same thing 100 times over, I would never have hit it as cleanly with my fist as I did on that occasion.

Now Hearts were a pretty good side at that time, with players like Andy Anderson, Alex Massie, Barney Battles, Tommy Walker and Jack, who had been in the 1928 Wembley Wizards side when with Queen's Park. They were a team that flattered to deceive. They had a number of good players, but I always felt that they were just a wee bit on the soft side, and when things got a bit physical they were liable to give more ground than they should.

Nonetheless on this occasion they were leading 3-1 at half-time and 4-1 with just 17 minutes to go. It looked as though we were about to suffer a most humiliating defeat on our own back-yard. Things looked fine early in the game when I scored just after five minutes. But Coutts scored twice and Battles scored before half-time, and then their outside-right Bobby Johnstone scored a fourth.

We decided we'd have to switch the team around in an effort to save the match, so Willie Nicholson was moved to left-back in place of Tommy Russell, who had been signed from Cowdenbeath. He moved forward and Jimmy Smith switched places with Jimmy Fleming, who had started the game at outside-right.

Well, I managed to score a second goal and then Jimmy Fleming got a third. We then found ourselves 4-3 down with four minutes to go when over came a hard, driven cross from the right. Whether it was from "Flem" or Smithie I don't recall. But I threw myself at the ball, realised I was going to miss it by a fraction with my head, so I got my left fist up and fairly punched that ball straight into the net past the startled and pretty stricken Jack Harkness. My hat-trick!

The referee was Hugh Watson of Glasgow, who had no doubts at all about the quality of my goal. However, many years later I met Hugh in Glasgow and he asked me if I had in fact punched the ball into the net. When I admitted I had, he said: "Well all I can say, Bob, is thanks for not admitting it after the game. It wouldn't have done me any good."

Jack Harkness, of course, never ever forgave me. Every time we would meet he would go into an act of stepping back away from me, throw his arms across his face and pretend he was protecting himself from a punch. I had played in the same Scotland team as Jack on five occasions, so we were really good friends, and as we got older and he became football correspondent of the *Sunday Post*, we would talk about the failure of Hearts to win a championship during these years and of course 'The Goal That Never Should Have Been'. But the point that day proved quite vital because in the end Rangers won the championship by a mere three points from Motherwell with Hearts in third place.

When I made my first-team debut for Rangers in April 1927, after my transfer from Airdrie, it was against Queen's Park in the first round of the Glasgow Cup at Ibrox. The Queen's goalie was none other than Jack Harkness. Jack had no happy memories of that game, because Rangers won 8-1. A bad experience for him considering he was at that time the Scotland 'keeper. I scored my first goal for Rangers in the 12th minute of that match, which happened to be Rangers' third, so the poor old Spiders were never really in the game at any point. Jimmy Fleming scored four, Andy Cunningham scored twice and Sandy Archibald got the other. The Rangers team that day was: Hamilton; Gray, McCandless; Meiklejohn, Shaw, Muirhead; Archibald, Cunningham, Fleming, McPhail, Morton. Our centre-half, Hugh Shaw, was a former Hibs player who was later transferred to Hearts and became manager of the famous Hibs side which had that exciting forward-line of Smith, Johnstone, Reilly, Turnbull and Ormond in the early 1950s.

My first "Old Firm" match came just a few days later in the semi-final of the Glasgow Cup. The only change in the Rangers side was Tully Craig at left-half for Tommy Muirhead. We beat Celtic 4-1 and I scored twice, with Fleming and Archibald scoring the others. I got rave notices from the Press the following day. I was treading on air. But not for long.

In the final we were beaten 6-3 by Partick Thistle after extra time with the Thistle centre-forward Sandy Hair scoring five. I managed to score again, with Alan Morton scoring twice. Mind you Rangers were a wee bit under strength as Archibald, Craig, Hamilton, Muirhead and Cunningham had all left with the Scotland team on a tour of Canada.

OK, so I had "conned" the referee in that match with Hearts but I had learned much earlier on that referees were a breed apart, and not all of their decisions were to be as generous as that of Hugh Watson. Now, I have never ever denied that I was a hard player to play against,

149

and I always made sure my opponents knew this. No one whacked me and got away with it, and referees tended to notice this little idiosyncrasy of mine. Yet the one and only time I was sent off during my career was after I had been sent sprawling on to the turf at Dundee. I didn't even get the chance to retaliate!

My protagonist was Colin McNab, the Dundee right-half, with whom I was to play alongside in a Scotland strip against England at Hampden in 1931, when we were to win 2-0. This was September 1928. Rangers were the champions and the Cup holders. We were the team to beat.

I have to say that McNab was a good player, and one who enjoyed the physical side of the game. He tackled with a zest that made you grit your teeth . . . mostly with pain. He was good enough to gain six caps for Scotland at at time when we had outstanding right-half-backs like Peter Wilson of Celtic, Alex Massie of Hearts, Jimmy Gibson of Aston Villa and of course our skipper Davie Meiklejohn.

As I lay there gritting my teeth in anger, while the Rangers trainer Jimmy Kerr tended to my bruised ankle, the referee, Tom Dougray, who came from my home town of Barrhead, trotted over. He looked at McNab and myself, pursed his lips and then sent us packing to the pavilion. I just couldn't believe it. I had been clearly fouled by McNab, who had been trying to prove throughout the game he was a harder man than I was — and had been winning! — and I had been injured, and awarded the free-kick. Yet I was being sent off for the first, and last, time in my career. I do admit that I had given McNab a rich mouthful of the language I had learned from Hughie Gallacher in my youth. I assumed that Dougray had heard the words and that I had been sent off for using foul and abusive language.

I didn't realise a dressing-room could be so lonely. Having a bath alone in the Dens Park pavilion with the game still going on was one of the worst experiences I've ever had. Every noise I made seemed to echo round the empty bathroom, and I just couldn't get rid of the feeling that I was the victim of a massive injustice. I hadn't even kicked McNab. Yet here I was alone in the bath. The only good news I got from the match was that Davie Meiklejohn had scored from the penalty spot to give us a 3-2 win.

There was no automatic suspension in those days. When you were sent off you were allowed to keep playing until you were called to appear before "the beaks" at the SFA headquarters, then in Carlton Place, overlooking the River Clyde.

Thus McNab and I duly appeared before the officials who sat in judgment of erring players during a season. When I was called before them I was asked if I knew what I had been charged with. There was considerable consternation when I told them that I did not. A copy of the referee's report had been sent to the Rangers manager, but Bill Struth had neglected to inform me of the charge or charges against me, though I had learned that Dougray had intimated that he had warned both McPhail and McNab earlier in the game.

Well, of course there was a great deal of shuffling of papers. I was then asked to leave the room for a few moments. When I returned I was told that I had been sent off because McNab and I had "adopted a fighting attitude". I told the officials that this was not only untrue, but was also impossible. "How could I adopt a fighting attitude, gentlemen, when I was lying on the ground being treated by the Rangers trainer? After all I had been fouled and a free-kick had been given against McNab." There was a bit more shuffling of papers here and I was again invited to leave the room. Eventually I was readmitted along with McNab. We were both told by the chairman of the committee that they didn't want to see us before them again and "to go back to your clubs and behave yourselves".

I later learned that the referee was furious that neither of us had been suspended. While Bill Struth was delighted with the committee's judgment he did not hide his anger at Dougray's decision to send me off. Struth told me: "If I have anything to do with it, that man Dougray won't referee another Rangers match." I have the feeling that Mr Dougray refereed fewer Rangers matches than was his right thereafter.

He was, of course, very much one of Scotland's top referees and was never impressed by the aggressive play of Meiklejohn and McPhail. He was constantly at our elbows during a game saying: "I'm watching you!" Shoulder charges were very much part and parcel of football in these pre-war days. Players accepted it — and the fans loved it. So "Meek" and I, and most of the top players who had the physique to dish it out, did so, and were prepared to be hit in return. I don't think a good shoulder charge ever did anyone any harm. But Dougray didn't like it. he hated the rough and tumble side of the game.

I never was one of Dougray's favourite players. I recall one typically hectic Celtic-Rangers match, when Dougray was referee, and the ball finished high up the slope of the terracing. While we were waiting for the ball to be thrown back a voice roared at me: "Hey, McPhail. You're nothing but a big tangerine-faced bastard." With a huge smile on his face, Dougray whispered to me: "There's someone who knows you!" Before I could get the chance to answer him, the same voice shouted: "And see you, Dougray. You're nothing but a wee frog-bellied bastard!" I quickly turned to him and said: "He obviously knows you too!"

Dougray did have a wee pot on him, which he tried to conceal under a white waistcoat, under his blue referee's jacket, so the voice was pretty accurate. Dougray and I both got a laugh at each other, the ball was thrown back and I got back to the business of helping Rangers beat Celtic.

Two of the toughest full-backs I ever played against were Findlay and Hamilton of St Mirren. You didn't need shinguards to play against these fellows, you needed sandbags. Both were eventually transferred to Armadale and as luck would have it Rangers were drawn to play against them in the first round of the Scottish Cup — at Armadale.

Rangers on shaky ground? Would the minnow swallow the whale? A Cup shock perhaps? The Press did the usual pre-match build-up while Hamilton, who was known in the trade as "Bull", was letting it be known that he would take a personal delight in "sorting out McPhail". This I didn't fancy one little bit, so I reported what I had heard to Bill Struth. Struth told the referee, A H Leishman of Falkirk, of the threats being bandied about by Hamilton, prior to the match. Leishman listened to Struth so well that Hamilton was sent off after just 15 minutes! So determined was Leishman to ensure a clean game that when Hamilton, who had a dreadful reputation, committed his first foul, he was off before he could utter a protest. Rangers won 7-1, I scored two of them, and felt that the ball players had been well and truly protected!

I'm convinced to this day that it was a refereeing decision that cost us the match in the second round of that 1931 Cup tournament. We had drawn Dundee at Ibrox, which delighted us. But unfortunately so much rain fell before the match that the ground took on the look of a paddy field. The conditions were terrible. There is no way the game should have been played but Mr J Thomson of Hamilton decreed otherwise, and we lost 2-1. Dundee simply adapted to the conditions better than we did. They cleverly kept the ball on their wings, while we stupidly tried to play our normal game and got ourselves bogged down in the water and mud which clogged up the middle of the field. Mind you, my direct opponent, Colin McNab, thoroughly enjoyed it. Didn't he just love those big sliding tackles in the mud!

15

When Motherwell Smashed the Monopoly

Rangers would have set a world record of nine successive championship wins from 1927 to 1935 if it hadn't been for Motherwell, one of the best footballing sides I ever played against during my years at Ibrox. They had been threatening to win the championship for the first time in their history for several years before they were finally successful in season 1931-32. No one, least of all Rangers, could grudge them this success.

Under the astute manager, John Hunter, they had just broken a Celtic-Rangers monopoly of the championship which had existed for 27 years, with their centre-forward Willie McFadyen setting an all-time scoring record of 52 league goals in 34 games, which still stands to this day. Willie, a real bustler of a centre-forward, beat Jimmy McGrory's then record of 49 goals in a season when he scored in the last minute against Cowdenbeath in a 3-0 win. He then raised the total to 52 with two goals in the last game of the season, against Clyde, to wrap up the League flag.

There wasn't a prouder man in the country than the Motherwell skipper Bobby Ferrier, who was then in his 14th season at Fir Park, and was one of the best left-wingers ever produced in Britain. What a left foot he had! In 626 league games for Motherwell, stretching from 1918 to 1937, Bobby scored 256 goals, most of them with that left peg of his. Two seasons prior to the championship success, Bobby had scored 32 goals in 27 league games, which is still a Scottish best for any winger playing in the top division. He had a vicious swerve on his shot, which he invariably managed to keep low, and which persistently beat 'keepers inside their near post. He was one of a number of really outstanding players Motherwell had at that time, and yet Bobby was not allowed to play for Scotland, because he had been born in Sheffield.

In many ways this was a tragedy. His father, who won two English championship medals with The Wednesday, now known, of course, as Sheffield Wednesday, in 1903 and 1904, was a Scot, as was Bobby's mother. Indeed he was taken north to the family home in Dumbarton when he was a mere six weeks old.

Though he was never allowed to challenge Alan Morton, Adam McLean, and Alex Troup for Scotland's left-wing position, he did play seven times for the Scottish Football League, though I never ever got the chance of playing alongside him. We seemed to avoid each other.

I should add that Celtic's manager, Willie Maley, went to look at Bobby when he got a Scottish Junior cap at the age of 17, when he played with the Glasgow Junior side, Petershill. Maley decided he wouldn't do. He was too one-footed! Maley didn't often make such mistakes.

Ferrier formed a brilliant left-wing partnership with George Stevenson, who was a stylish, skilful player and a master at hitting the delayed pass. They had a telepathic understanding, which was the despair of right-backs, with Stevenson cutting the ball behind the full-back for Ferrier to run on to and shoot or pass. Exciting to watch — so long as you weren't playing against them. It was a partnership that was constantly being compared with McPhail and Morton.

Their championship-winning team was McClory; Dowall, Ellis; Wales, Craig, Telfer; Murdoch, McMenemy, McFadyen, Stevenson and Ferrier, with only little Johnny Murdoch failing to play at least 30 of the 38 league games. They beat us by five points and the statistics from that season are interesting, because both teams scored exactly 118 goals. Here they are:

	Played	Won	Lost	Drawn	For	Against	Pts.
Motherwell	38	30	2	6	118	31	66
Rangers	38	28	5	5	118	42	61

During that season Motherwell had 17 shut-outs, lost just one goal in 11 of their games, and lost two games — 1-0 to Kilmarnock and 1-0 to Rangers.

Hunter, who had signed eight of this team from the Junior ranks, had worked hard at getting the ideal blend. All his strong players were in defence, with a good contrast at wing-half where Hughie Wales, my direct opponent, was a wee hard-working grafter who soon let you know he was on the field. The left-half, Willie Telfer, was a clever player, who used the ball well and of course fed Stevenson and Ferrier in front of him.

But the fellow behind them was something else! His name was Ben Ellis, a Welshman, who would have kicked his grannie into the stand if it meant getting to the ball. Ben only seemed to see the ball during a game. If someone happened to get in the way of it, then that was their misfortune. I was always very thankful that I played on the other side of the field from Mr Ellis. I think it helped to prolong my career. He was some character.

Of course he could play a bit, and proved it on the three occasions he played for his country against Scotland. He finished on the winning side each time! In his first appearance against the Scots in 1932 at Tynecastle the Welsh went on the rampage and won 5-2, after leading 4-0 at half-time. Wee Jimmy Crawford, Scotland's right-winger from Queen's Park, did not have one of his better games. A year later, when I should have skippered the Scots side at Cardiff, but had to pull out with injury, Wales won again, with Ben at left-back. This time the score was 3-2. Our outside-right on that occasion was Frank McGurk from Birmingham City. Ben must have done a good job on him, as it was McGurk's one and only cap. Bobby Main of Rangers was his direct opponent in the 1937 match at Cardiff, when I was at inside-left. We were beaten 2-1. Bobby didn't say too much after the game but sadly I have to add that, like McGurk, it was Bobby's one and only appearance for Scotland. So it was a nice hat-trick of successes for Ben, wasn't it? A real demolisher of a defender and no mistake.

Big Alan Craig wasn't too gentle either. He was the classic stopper centre-half. No nonsense. He just made sure that he cleared his lines as quickly as he could, even if his direction was a wee bit off at times.

Murdoch I knew well, because he and I played together in the Airdrie reserve side, where he developed the knack of "poaching" goals. He was a smart wee player, who could make openings for himself by reading the game properly and who fitted in well to the Motherwell system of play. His inside-right was Johnny McMenemy, who would have been considered a midfield player today. Always comfortable on the ball, Johnny would lie back and make his passes do the work.

Willie McFadyen? What a work-horse. Willie hustled and bustled defenders, rumbled them up, and battled for every ball up front. The Motherwell players told me at the end of that season that Willie should have scored another 20 goals with the chances that were created for him. But 52 wasn't bad, was it?

Early in that season it looked as though Motherwell might well be on course for a League and Cup double, as they knocked Celtic out of the

Scottish Cup in the third round at Fir Park, beating them 2-0 with goals from Murdoch and Ferrier. But Rangers stopped them in their tracks. We beat them in the fourth round at Ibrox 2-0, before a crowd of 88,000, and I just loved the morning paper headline the following day: MOTHERWELL'S MCPHAIL—URE IN CUP! They don't write them like that any more.

I had had a really good game and had scored the second goal which finished Motherwell. I had sent Jimmy Fleming away on the right wing with a long pass, and then sprinted into the box for his return. He hit it exactly where I wanted it, and from 12 yards I didn't give Alan McClory a chance of getting anywhere near the shot. Our first goal was scored by our inside-right, a laddie named Jimmy Murray, who came from Saltcoats. It was the only time he ever played for Rangers in a Cup tie, so he must have treasured that goal all his life.

Well, that set us up. We beat Hamilton Accies 5-2 in the semi-final and then beat Kilmarnock in the final after a replay. You know, maybe we did Motherwell a favour in knocking them out that early, as they were able to concentrate solely on the championship, which their manager wanted so dearly.

For the first time in their history Motherwell had ended as runners-up in the championship in 1927, finishing five points adrift of Rangers. The following two seasons they finished third, and then in 1930 they finished runners-up once again to Rangers, before being third the following year. So the consistency was there to suggest they were potential champions, despite the stranglehold Celtic and Rangers seemed to have on Scottish football. Indeed, in eight successive seasons — 1927 to 1934 — they finished no lower than third, which suggests that wee John Hunter, their manager, wasn't so far behind Bill Struth, Willie Maley and my first boss at Airdrie, Willie Orr, in the art of finding and moulding good players into outstanding teams.

Motherwell had good reason to enjoy their celebration dinner in the old Grosvenor Hotel, near Glasgow's Central rail station, after their fine championship win. They must have been a team wondering if they were ever going to win a major trophy.

The previous season had ended in a total disaster for them, at Hampden Park. There they were playing good football, in control of the final against Celtic and leading 2-0 with just nine minutes to go. Then it all started to go wrong. Charlie Napier, at outside-left for Celtic, took a free-kick which had to be dangerous as "happy-feet", as he was known, could bend the ball in flight, and he could hit it hard.

The kick was perfect and there was Jimmy McGrory to whip the ball past big Alan McClory.

So it was backs to the wall for the Motherwell defence as the crowd of 105,000 (or most of them) roared on the Celtic team. With just one minute remaining, the Parkhead right-winger Bertie Thomson, of the soup-bowl haircut, took possession on the wing. To the surprise and frustration of the crowd he held the ball, and refused to be rushed into a quick cross. He turned one way and then another, before despatching a high lob into the goal area. McClory could see it all the way, and moved out confidently to pull it out of the air. For reasons which he was never able to fully explain, Alan Craig suddenly made a lunge at the ball with his head, to send it into the net past his astonished 'keeper. What a disaster for any defender!

Motherwell had had the Cup in their hands, with Peter Craigmyle looking at his watch, when Celtic got themselves that dramatic last gasp equaliser to the horror of Craig. The teams in that Scottish Cup final of 1931 were: *Motherwell*: McClory; Johnman, Hunter; Wales, Craig, Telfer; Murdoch, McMenemy, McFadyen, Stevenson, Ferrier. *Celtic*: J Thomson; Cook, McGonagle; Wilson, J McStay, Geatons; R Thomson, A Thomson, McGrory, Scarff, Napier.

The teams were unchanged for the replay, when the fighting Cup spirit of Celtic prevailed. The Motherwell defenders looked uncertain and hesitant throughout as Jimmy McGrory and Bertie Thomson scored two goals apiece in a 4-2 victory. Murdoch and Stevenson had scored for Motherwell, whose dreams had been shattered.

Two years later they made the Scottish Cup final once more. Again they met Celtic. This time a replay wasn't required. Celtic won 1-0, with the sheer persistence of Bertie Thomson setting up the goal and, of course, Jimmy McGrory putting his name on it just two minutes after the interval.

To appear in three finals and lose each one must be a heartbreaking experience, but it happened to Hughie Wales and George Stevenson. They were back at Hampden again in the final of 1939. Clyde whipped them 4-0.

So the championship win of 1932 was very special to Motherwell. They were in fact the only team outside Celtic and Rangers to win the championship from 1905 to 1948. During that period Celtic had won the league flag 15 times and Rangers 20. There was no Monopolies Commission in those early days!

The 66 league points won by Motherwell that season is still the Fir

Park record, and while it would have been nice to have been a member of a Rangers team setting a world record of nine successive championship wins, I don't think any of us at Ibrox were too cut up at Motherwell's season of success.

It was a Bulgarian team, CDNA Sofia who eventually set a world best of nine successive championship wins from 1954 to 1962. A record equalled by Jock Stein's Celtic during 1966 to 1974, during which time, of course, they became not only the first British side to reach the final of the European Cup but the first British side to win it.

I just welcome this opportunity of paying tribute to the marvellous Motherwell side of my time, when their clever, attacking play deserved much more success than a single championship win. We always had a good game with them. There was rarely any rancour in our meetings, even though we had our share of hard, physical players. Indeed I recall John Hunter, their manager, making an analysis of the difference between his inside-left George Stevenson and myself. He told me: "Geordie's got the finesse you don't have, and you've got the physical strength I wish he had." He wasn't far wrong.

16

When I Stayed Away from the Boardroom

Around my 80th birthday I was made a Life Member of Rangers Football Club, which assured me of a seat in the directors' box at any match during the season. It's a privilege I'm proud to possess and, of course, take full advantage of because I still love this game of football.

Many years ago when the late Matt Taylor was the club's chairman I was offered a directorship of the club. But I refused, even though my former team-mates George Brown and Alan Morton, who made the left-wing triangle with me in many of Rangers' successes, did become board members. My reason was straightforward. I did not want to be involved in the politics of the game. I was happy in the role I had been given by Bill Struth when I had decided my playing days were over, and that was, I suppose, counsellor to the reserve team.

My job for almost 40 years was to travel with the reserves on a Saturday, give them encouragement, give them advice, and report to the manager what progress there was among the younger players. It was a duty I enjoyed. Struth felt that his young players needed someone to look after them whom they could respect and would recognise as a former player who could speak from experience and the knowledge of what is needed to be a success at Ibrox.

He decided I was the right man for the job, put me on the pay-roll, and I'm still getting paid to this day. Since the days of Struth I've worked with Scot Symon, Davie White, Willie Waddell, Jock Wallace, and John Greig. I've seen hundreds of players come and go and I hope that I helped most of them understand and enjoy the game better.

As a director of the club I would have become a public figure. I would have been required to attend board meetings, become heavily involved with the organisation of football, become part of the controversial issues which must always feature in a major club like

159

Rangers and, of course, become the ideal target for people who want to find out what goes on behind the scenes at Ibrox.

I have been able to say, in all honesty, that I do not know what goes on behind the scenes at Ibrox, because I have never had any real status within the club. I have never been a director, and I have never even owned a share, which debars me from attending the annual general meeting of the club. My escape from my business was spending Saturday afternoons helping the young Rangers reserves, reporting to the manager on a Thursday evening and giving him my opinions of the players.

Manager? I never wanted to be a manager of any club. When there were rumours that Bob McPhail might be the next manager of St Mirren during the war years, my wife Jessie said to me: "If you become a manager, you'll lose a wife!" What she was really saying was that now that my days as a player were over she wanted to settle down and have a real family life, which included children who would see their father every evening. She was right, of course. Football had been good to us. Indeed it set us up for life. But Jessie didn't want it to become our life. She didn't want her husband coming home at all hours of the night with the worries that go with managing a football club, the constant ringing of the phone, the publicity, the pressures on your time to attend functions. She had had enough of it when I was a player with Rangers. I agreed.

Every manager I've ever spoken to over the past 65 years or so has said the same thing: "Nothing beats playing." After all, I wasn't looking for a job. I had one. I was running an electrical equipment supply company, and the business was proving successful. Why should I chase ulcers?

Now, never at any time did I pick a Rangers reserve side. The manager of the period did that. My job was to make the most of the lads I was given, point out the little mistakes they had made in the previous game, give them a bit of direction and impress upon them the disciplinary code of the club.

As a manager I would have been much more strict. I'm too much of a perfectionist. I see too many flaws in players. I would have expected them all to play like Davie Meiklejohn, Alan Morton, Sandy Archibald, Tully Craig and George Brown. And of course that would have been impossible. Struth got it right. A chip off the old block looking after the kids.

I just don't have the space here to detail all the players I spoke to in the reserve side over so many years but obviously one or two do spring to mind.

I recall the early days of Davy Wilson, a wee fair-haired winger who joined us from Baillieston Juniors in 1956. Here was a confident wee fellow who wasn't afraid to get himself into the penalty box and look for goals. Like Alan Morton he was a natural right-footed player, and scored a lot of his goals by cutting inside the full-back and letting fly.

I knew he would make it, and it didn't surprise me at all that he established himself as a Scotland player and won 22 caps.

Jim Forrest and his cousin Alex Willoughby joined us in 1961 as a couple of fresh-faced kids who showed tremendous enthusiasm in the reserve side. But after a few games Jim came to me and said: "Mr McPhail, I don't think you should play me at inside-forward. I just don't have the ability for that position. I don't think I have the ball control that is needed. I think I'd be a better player at centre-forward where I know I can get goals." I liked the honesty of this young fellow, so thereafter he played at centre-forward. He did score a lot of goals and formed a pretty lethal partnership with his cousin. It wasn't long before he made the league side, and in 1964 he scored 56 goals in 50 games to set a club record.

Around this time we had wee Willie Henderson who came from Lanarkshire. He called everybody "Sur". Here was a remarkable bundle of natural talent which needed no advice. He was fast, strong, and could change direction without a break in pace. He was a devastating wee winger, but there were times when I felt Willie did things on the field then wondered how he did them.

Nobody wearied when Willie was in the dressing-room. He was a great favourite with everyone and of course thrived on the skilful service he got from Ian McMillan when he became an established first-team player.

By this time Scot Symon was the Rangers manager. I remember him being transferred as a player from Portsmouth to Rangers for £1,000 the day after we beat Arsenal 1-0 at Ibrox in September 1938. He had already played with Dundee, so he was an experienced player, signed to replace George Brown, and good enough to be capped three months later against Hungary at Hampden, where goals from Torry Gillick, Tommy Walker and Andy Black gave the Scots a good 3-1 win.

Scot played behind me in my final season at Ibrox. He was a hard player and a great passer of the ball. He drove the ball hard to your feet. He always seemed to deliver the ball on the ground, making it easy for

Sharing a joke with former Rangers skipper and manager John Greig. Like myself, John won six Scottish Cup medals with Rangers, and was as great an influence to the Ibrox squad in his playing days as Davie Meiklejohn was when I played. He was my kind of player.

you to take quick control and do what you had to do with it.

When he replaced Struth as manager in 1954, after taking East Fife to two League Cup wins, and then Preston North End to the final of the FA Cup, he wasted no time in establishing his authority at Ibrox. And he did well. In his 13 years as the Rangers manager he won the League Championship six times, the Scottish Cup five times and the Scottish League Cup four times out of five from 1960 to 1965.

Twice he took Rangers to the final of the European Cup Winners Cup, yet in 1967 the Ibrox board of directors branded him a failure and sacked him. To say I was shocked was putting it mildly. I was horrified. How could the club treat a man like Symon so shabbily? I knew him well — very well, and I knew the man worked morning, noon and night for Rangers. His passion for the club was undeniable.

In many respects he was a loner. He never sought to make friends, and he was always wary of strangers. I would see him every Thursday night when he would relax and talk about the reserve players. He was no fool. He knew there was pressure being exerted on his chairman John Lawrence and the rest of the Ibrox board of that time during the mid to late '60s from people who were jealous at the success Celtic were enjoying under the leadership of Jock Stein.

A sequence of events brought the end for Scot. The Scottish Cup defeat from wee Berwick Rangers, the defeat from Bayern Munich in the final of the European Cup Winners Cup in Nuremberg and Celtic winning the European Cup in Lisbon the same year. The Rangers board of directors, who had voted unanimously to ask for his resignation, sent an accountant, Alex McBain, to talk severence money with Scot. He wouldn't resign, and later announced to the Press that he had been sacked. At that time Rangers were top of the league, and undefeated.

I had been pretty sure that Scot Symon would have finished his time in football as a working director of the club, perhaps administrative manager, a job he was later to do so well with Partick Thistle. He was the last of the managers in a pin-stripe suit. The track-suit coaches were taking over. Tradition was tottering. Symon was only the third Rangers manager in the history of the club, following Willie Wilton and Bill Struth. To give him the sack was no credit to Rangers. I phoned him immediately offering him what comfort I could. It took him many months to get over it, and it was eight years before he ever set foot in Ibrox again.

I found it all very distressing. I also found it very difficult to understand the appointment of Davie White as manager. Here was a young man, imbued with enthusiasm and ambition, being asked to build a team to compete with the greatest Celtic team in history, and against a manager who was to become the most successful ever in British football. He was thrown into the deep end, with very little chance of success.

Rangers only began to recover when Willie Waddell gave up journalism and took over. He swept through the club with a vengeance, brought streamlined organisation into effect, and made it clear to everyone that he was running Rangers. And that was what was needed at that time. Winning the European Cup Winners Cup in Barcelona,

According to my records Alan Morton and I played together on the Rangers left wing a total of 189 League and Cup games over six seasons and on six occasions for Scotland. As the picture shows we remained close together for many years later in the best interest of Rangers, Alan as a director and me as mentor to the reserve team.

beating Moscow Dynamo 3-2, in 1972, only proved the effectiveness of Waddell's leadership.

The changes since then have been quite dramatic with players like Graeme Souness, Chris Woods, Terry Butcher, Graham Roberts, Trevor Francis, Jan Bartram and Mark Walters all pulling on a Rangers strip. These fellows earn more in a week than I did in an entire season in the 1930s, but there is no envy on my part. I was well paid at

I've just explained to former Rangers chairman John Paton and former manager Jock Wallace that there is no way they are borrowing any of the medals I won during my playing career. "If you want any medals, win them yourselves," I told them. But I did allow them to look at them.

Ibrox throughout my entire career with the club, when Bill Struth paid out more to his players than they could get from any other club in Britain.

When I got married in June 1933 I was able to buy my house with ready cash. My John Lawrence-built house in 12 Etive Drive, Giffnock, cost me £650, which was a lot of money in those days. But how many players today could buy a home with ready money?

I also had a car; first a Morris-Cowley bottle-nosed sports model, and then a square-nosed Morris. So financially I had no complaints. Before I got married I used to drive a motorbike with sidecar and take my fiancée Jessie from Barrhead down to Largs for a run. Come to think of it, it couldn't have been much fun while we were travelling, with Jessie stuffed inside the sidecar with poor visibility and little air.

The motorbike was a hand-me-down from my brother Malcolm. I bought my first car from a garage near Strathbungo Station near the Gorbals district of Glasgow. No licence was required in those days, so with some difficulty I drove it to a garage in Barrhead where my friend Bobby Paton was a mechanic. I managed to stop the car, but I didn't know how to stop the engine. Out came Bobby with a cynical look on his face to demonstrate how easy it was to turn off the ignition. Right there the big-time car owner felt a little squashed!

Maybe I had been too eager to follow in the footsteps of Tommy McInally of Celtic, who had been driving about Barrhead in a Citröen, and was always giving people lifts, including myself. He had a gallus wee friend called Gibby Murray who decided to test Tommy's knowledge of cars, which was as good as mine. He lifted the bonnet of his Citröen, put a dead sparrow on his engine, then closed the bonnet again. He then shouted to Tommy: "What about a run in your car?" "Delighted," said Tommy, but before he could get into the driving seat Murray asked to see under the bonnet, as he had never seen a car engine. Up came the bonnet, and there lay the dead sparrow. McInally couldn't work out how a sparrow had got under his bonnet and then breathed its last on top of his engine. When he found out, Murray and McPhail made sure they were a safe distance away.

To own a car and your own home before the war you just had to be earning good money. My wages were £8 a week, plus a £2 bonus for a win (which was almost every week!) and a legal bonus of £20 for winning the Scottish Cup (which we did fairly regularly). What was the illegal bonus from Bill Struth? Now did I say there was one?

17

Turnberry

Turnberry Hotel is a place of luxury and leisure on the Ayrshire coast which provides a quite spectacular backcloth to the Turnberry golf courses, where some of the world's major tournaments have taken place. Who can forget the 1977 Open Championship for instance when Tom Watson and Jack Nicklaus set the course ablaze in the final round with Watson winning by a stroke after both had birdied the final hole? Turnberry never looked better that particular week. The hotel, with its white walls and red roofs, provides a breathtaking panoramic view of the Ailsa Craig bird sanctuary, which rises 1,114 feet out of the Firth of Clyde, and has a rock formation from which the very best curling stones are made.

Bill Struth loved the place.

Our manager would take us to this propitious property three or four times during a season. We would take the train from Glasgow, which is 50 miles to the north, to Girvan, five miles south of Turnberry, and then take the local train to Turnberry itself.

He chose Turnberry as our regular retreat because, first of all, he loved the place and secondly because it was so isolated. He wanted to rest his players, freshen them, give them a change from the daily routine at Ibrox, and encourage what Tommy Muirhead called "camaraderie". We never ever had any interference or interruption from supporters, simply because it was an extremely difficult place to get to in those days, unless you possessed a car.

Struth timed his visits meticulously. He would judge when he considered Rangers would have an "easy" home game, and then arrange for us to stay in the hotel on the Saturday night, Sunday and Monday prior to the so-called Saturday walk-over. He always seemed to get it right.

While our manager would never admit it publicly, he happened to enjoy playing golf on the championship course, and first thing Sunday morning he would be out there with his regular partner, club chairman Bailie Joe Buchanan, lining up against the club's best golfers, Davie Meiklejohn and Alan Morton.

The management always won. It was all about bisques. For those who don't play golf, a bisque is a floating stroke conceded in the form of a handicap in match play. The player can take any of his bisques at any hole he decides. He can take it after he holes out on the green, provided he tells his partner he's taking the stroke before leaving the green. Which means if both players take a 5 at a hole, and one decides to take one of the bisques he is due, then he is the winner of that hole.

Meek and Alan always had to concede these bisques to Struth and the chairman. And I think the number of bisques given depended on how well Struth and his partner were playing. If it looked as though the players were going to win, then Meek and the wee man would be told that they hadn't offered enough bisques. Well of course Meek and Morton had decided long ago that it wasn't really prudent for them to win this regular challenge match. They were quite happy to lose with dignity.

We were all encouraged to play the game, because Struth, always the fitness fanatic, insisted the players got out there and filled their lungs with the pure air from the sea breezes. Tully Craig was adamant. He thought golf was "a stupid bloody game" and stubbornly refused to put his hands anywhere near a club. But there was no chance of a long lie for Tully or a leisurely morning cup of coffee in the lounge with his feet up. Struth got him out on the course along with the rest of us, with orders to walk along the edge of the course close to the sandy beach, and all the way to the lighthouse, at Turnberry Point, which is 80 feet high, and walk all the way back. Tully knew that Struth would watch him from the course.

Walk? We would walk until we were close to exhaustion each day. Struth's favourite stroll was from the Turnberry Hotel towards Girvan. He would then head left on a road through the fields, sweep round behind the hotel, and come back close to the beach at Maidens, which is an old fishing village. We would then leg it along the road to the hotel. We would follow him like sheep, in twos and threes.

Now this walk would always take place before dinner, with Struth insisting that we all do deep breathing while we walked. You could always hear the moans from Sandy Archibald. He would say in a loud voice: "I thought we came down to this place for a rest."

Struth would reply: "Archibald, keep your wind for Saturday, you'll need it!"

It is interesting to me that the current Rangers manager, Graeme Souness, not only discourages his players from playing golf, but has banned the sport altogether during the football season. He reckons it doesn't do their legs any good at all. Tully Craig would certainly have agreed with him.

There was always a fair bit of horse-play on these three-day "rest cures" of Bill Struth. My regular room-mate on these visits was big Jimmy Smith. On one occasion when we returned to our room after dinner, we found the place a shambles. Sheets, bedclothes, pillows, chairs, and anything that could be moved — and that included beds — had been turned upside down.

Just as we entered the door, we spotted a leg going out the window, so Jimmy, being the younger man, gave chase. Out the window he went, not realising that there was a steep, grassy embankment outside. It also happened to be very wet. Jimmy slipped, went down the embankment head over heels, got himself covered in mud and rain-water, and if I remember correctly finished in a flower bed.

When I realised what had happened to him, I immediately closed the window, and nipped out into the corridor to tell the rest of the team. We then all ran to the front of the hotel to await the bedraggled Smithie, who staggered up to the front door, a horrible sight, looking for blood. He got a tremendous cheer from the lads, and there in the background was Bill Struth laughing louder than most.

Smithie got his own back. On another occasion I was given room 37, if I remember, when I booked in. I went upstairs, put my belongings on my bed and rushed downstairs for a cup of tea. When I went back upstairs my room had disappeared! I could find rooms 36 and 38, but no 37. The rest of the lads came out to help me look for the room, including my deadpan room-mate Smith.

"I don't understand this," said Jimmy. "You must have been given the wrong number on the key."

Eventually I went downstairs, got the manager, and explained that I had a key with room number 37, but there didn't appear to be such a room. Upstairs we went, along the corridor, where the manager stopped beside a huge wardrobe, and said to me: "Sir, your room is behind this wardrobe!" Smith and Dougie Gray had manhandled this huge piece of furniture from the corner of the corridor to cover my bedroom door. It was a perfect fit, and made me look the perfect ass of the week. Jimmy Smith still reminds me of that escapade to this very day.

Smith, a marvellous centre-forward who was so nimble on his feet, was always the joker in the pack. I recall him rendering George Brown speechless during a match, when George put him through on the right with a really good pass, and then ran into the penalty area to take the return. Instead of returning the ball to George, Jimmy tried a shot from a tight angle and hit the side net. An exasperated Brown shouted at him: "Why didn't you do the simple thing?"

Replied Smith: "Christ, there's nothing more simple than hitting the side net, is there?"

Jerry Dawson and Smith tried to sort me out one day after training at Ibrox. Both were having a whale of a time in the bathroom, turning the huge hose on everyone who went into the tub. Naturally they were hosing down everyone with cold water. I could hear clearly the commotion from the dressing-room. I shouted through the door: "Right lads, steady up. I'm coming through to the treatment room, and I don't want to get my clothes wet."

There was a bit of a silence for a few seconds, then I heard the hose being turned off. Smithie shouted: "Right, on you come Bob, we'll let you through now."

I immediately stripped off, put on Jerry's shirt which was hanging up with the rest of his clothes on a peg close to the door, pulled on a pair of training shorts and went through the door. Immediately I was doused with the water from the hose, to the great hilarity of jokers Smith and Dawson.

They then began to wonder why I just stood there and grinned. Dawson then looked at me and said: "You rotten bugger, that's my good shirt your wearing!" Smith laughed more than I did.

Only recently Jimmy reminded me of the time we played Bruels, an American side during our 1930 tour of America, in Cleveland under floodlights. When you kicked the ball up in the air, it was almost impossible to see it, because the floodlights were really large lanterns and were only about 50 feet above the ground. During the game Jimmy came over to me and said: "Bob, I'm playing against two centre-halfs here. I beat one fellow, then found myself facing another fellow I hadn't seen before. I think they've got too many men on the field."

Earlier Jimmy had heard the American coach shout on one of his players to come off the field, to allow a substitute on. The player, who was a Scot from Denny, turned to Jimmy and said: "There's no way, I'm going off. I always wanted to play against Rangers, and I'm staying on." He did.

I then suggested that we get the ball kicked well out of play so that we could count the number of players who were playing against us. So it was agreed that when Jimmy got a long clearance from our 'keeper, Tom Hamilton, he should whack the ball as it dropped and get it out of the playing area near the corner flag.

Sure enough a clearance from Hamilton dropped right at Jimmy's feet some minutes later. He took a vicious swipe at the ball on the turn and, would you believe, sent it flying straight into the back of the opposition net! A tremendous goal. Jimmy reminds me to this day that I gave him a roasting for not kicking the ball out of play. When we did manage to count the number of American players on the field, there were 17! When the substitutes came on, the other players just refused to go off.

Jimmy scored 18 goals on that tour, but that goal against Bruels was perhaps the most spectacular he ever scored in his life.

There is little doubt in my mind that our mid-season breaks to Turnberry and those close season tours to America were of inestimable value to Rangers as a club. They told us that nothing was too good for the Rangers players. At that time Turnberry had the best hotel in Scotland, so that's where we should have our breaks. It cost the club a lot of money, but they got it all back with the success we had in these days.

We didn't realise it but we were being slowly and gradually educated in how to conduct ourselves in public, how to handle publicity, how to behave, good manners, how to dress and how one should conduct oneself at the dinner table. Struth was making discipline a habit, on and off the field. If we could learn to live like gentlemen in places like Turnberry and the best hotels in Canada, America and wherever we happened to play in Europe, then there was no reason why we shouldn't behave like gentlemen every day of the week.

He even made golf lessons available for us at Turnberry. I remember Jimmy Smith's first-ever swipe at a golf ball. He was getting a lesson from the pro, who had hit a good drive, to give him an idea of what the swing was all about. Jimmy teed up the ball, took a wild swipe at the ball and sent it 20 yards further than the professional! Beginner's luck? It certainly was, but to this day Jimmy still tries to get a round or two at Ralston Golf Club, near Paisley, and has been as low as seven handicap.

171

I should add that we got ourselves a very special Rangers supporter during our times at Turnberry — Jack Buchanan, the sophisticated song-and-dance man from Helensburgh, who became a Hollywood star. Jack, very much a contemporary of Fred Astaire, who worked with great names like Bob Hope, Bing Crosby and Maurice Chevalier, always stayed at Turnberry when he was appearing in a musical in Glasgow. He even treated us to a very special soft-shoe shuffle one evening. The man had a lot of style. He and Bill Struth seemed to get along very well. But then "Mr" Struth wasn't without some style himself.

18

Football Cannot Fly Without Wings

Why oh why have the coaches and managers in recent years taken so much excitement and entertainment out of football by killing off the natural winger? Is it fear of defeat? Is it the fear of losing their job? Or is there an obsession throughout Europe, in particular, that most of the modern game must be played in the middle of the field?

I can only look back in anguish at names like Sandy Archibald and Alan Morton, Willie Waddell and Billy Liddell, Paddy Connolly and Adam McLean, Stan Matthews and Tom Finney, Gordon Smith and Willie Ormond, Willie Henderson and Davy Wilson, Jimmy Johnstone and Bobby Lennox and the wingers of the 1924 Airdrie Cup-winning side, Jimmy Reid and Jimmy Sommerville.

What excitement these gentlemen generated when they got the ball at their feet. The whole game would suddenly come alight with the roar of the crowd as a winger took off down the touchline, with defenders bracing themselves for the crossed ball and forwards picking out their places in the penalty area to make contact.

It rarely happens today. The modern game and my game of 60 years ago is so different. Two different games. I've seen it slowly deteriorate into a battle for supremacy in the middle of the field, where so many players have become masters of the square pass which has become a Saturday afternoon alternative to the sleeping pill.

For me, as a spectator, it has become a game of frustration and fussiness instead of the basic strategy of the game which is to go out and try and score more goals than your opponent.

Admittedly the rewards are higher today, but I do not think that players are any fitter , that the play is any faster or the whole ambiance of the game any better.

Even in my day trainers and managers were saying "the ball is made

173

round to go round" and "the fastest thing on the field is the ball". This hasn't changed. But because most teams have declared wingers as dead as the Dodo bird, use only two or three forwards, and pile everyone else behind them, the game has suffered sadly as a spectacle.

I found it quite stimulating to see Mark Walters come into the Rangers team from English football in 1987 and give the crowd a glimpse into the past with some good old-fashioned wing play. The crowd loved it when he turned on his "double-shuffle" to mesmerise his opponent on the wing, and then whip the ball across goal with either foot.

Every time he gets the ball you can sense the crowd being roused in expectation. And when he beats the full-back, the cheers become a roar, as he lines up his cross, or in some cases a shot at the target.

Now, didn't the crowd respond exactly the same when Sandy Archibald or Willie Waddell or wee Jimmy Johnstone took possession? Of course they did. And this is what is being lost to the game today.

Possession football is fine, if it is positive, but for many of the players I've watched over the past 15 years or so it has become the easy option. They hold it, then hit the ball square, or indeed pass it back 40 yards to their 'keeper. Why? Firstly because they have no wingers to find — Walters is almost an exception in Scotland — the centre-forward or main striker has two defenders covering him, and they are not encouraged to take on an opponent before making a pass.

The fan who pays his money each week wants to be entertained. He wants to be excited. And there is nothing more exciting in this game of football than the goalmouth incident. The public want to see goals and more goals, not the square pass into oblivion.

In my day the hardest-working players on the field were the inside-forwards and half-backs. We were the work-horses, shuttling up and down the field throughout 90 minutes without respite. We had no hiding place.

We had to learn that the greatest asset you could develop was the early pass. Graeme Souness, the present Rangers manager has it, David Meiklejohn had it, Scott Symon had it and so too did Tully Craig. The ability to make the ball do the work, for as I said the fastest thing on the field will always be the ball.

The player who can hit the ball with stunning accuracy without stopping it seems to be few and far between these days. Pre-war they seemed to be ten a penny. Apart from the men I've already mentioned there were none better at hitting the early pass than my first Rangers

174

skipper Tommy Muirhead, Peter Wilson of Celtic, Bob Bennie who played with me at Airdrie, the peerless Patsy Gallacher and Alex Thomson of Celtic.

If you stop the ball, you stop the game. Wingers keep the game flowing. Shouldn't we all be having a hard look at the type of game we're offering to the general public? Do they really want 4-4-2, 4-3-3, and 5-4-1 formations? I think not.

The game appears to be faster today, because the ball, which is now water resistant and remains constantly at a weight of one pound, is lively, the playing surfaces are better because of vastly improved drainage, and boots and gear are lighter.

In my day the ball absorbed water and on a wet day it became a ton weight. When you got your head to crosses when the going was heavy, you were in danger of being concussed. Often I actually saw stars or strange black spots after making contact with a cross from Sandy Archibald. And if you didn't make proper contact — ouch!

I think we were as fit as the present-day player, because we worked just as hard at our game. Though I was 5ft 10 inches in height and was known as a hard player, my weight was never more than 11st 3lbs throughout my career.

With the amount of work I was expected to do, there was no way I could put on weight. Indeed my problem was making sure I didn't lose any. My mother always made sure I got my porridge and eggs in the morning and some wholesome home-made soup after training each day. We may not have had the same varied menu, organised by dieticians, which the players of today get, but I don't remember any player of my generation dying of malnutrition! We were fit. We had to be, and I think we had to be more creative, more direct and more skilful in what we had to do.

Every team used the same formation, a 2-3-5, which meant you had two full-backs who never ventured over the half-way line, whose specific job was to stop the wingers getting past them to get over their crosses. The centre-half took on the centre-forward man to man, the half-backs took on the inside-forwards in the same way. Every player on the field had a direct opponent, and rarely if ever would you switch your position.

I don't think I ever "spelled" Alan Morton on the wing in all the years I played with him. He was a specialist, an artist, so why should I change with him? He certainly couldn't do my job as the work-horse inside-forward expected to defend and expected to score goals.

The crowds loved those man to man head-on confrontations. Dougie Gray against Adam McLean, Peter McGonagle against Sandy Archibald, Willie McStay against Alan Morton, Jimmy Simpson against Jimmy McGrory, Peter Wilson against Bob McPhail, and so on. This has been lost in the tortuous tactics of the current game, where the object seems to have shifted towards preventing the opposition playing instead of chasing goals.

If the game has changed, the fans haven't. They still have the same passion as they had in my day. They still want to see Rangers, Celtic, Hibs, Hearts and all the other teams they support win. They want to see great individuals and great individual touches, they live in controversy and argument, and they love nothing better than the well-struck shot or brilliant header which hits the back of the net.

I've played or watched this great game of ours for well over 60 years and I've seen all the subtle changes — and some not so subtle — throughout these years. And I've learned that players like Meiklejohn, Souness, Jim Baxter, Waddell, Archibald, Morton, Greig, McGrory, Ian McMillan, Patsy Gallacher and many other players in this class, could have played at any period in the history of our game with outstanding success, simply because they were all great players.

It troubles me sometimes that some young players never seem to improve, and some neglect to work harder at their game. I recall when I was a very young player with Airdrie I used to marvel at the way the Motherwell inside-right Willie Rankin managed to control a ball with his chest.

Any time I used my chest to try and get an awkward bouncing ball or high lob under control it seemed to bounce off my ribs. I then realised that Rankin would stand back from the ball, pull his chest in and raise his shoulders, therefore allowing the ball to roll into his body and down towards his feet. I practised this in training in the school ground opposite Ibrox in the mornings, until I had mastered it. I found I could always learn something new in the game in almost every game I played. And I really never ever stopped learning.

I hope that the emergence of a winger like Mark Walters is a healthy sign for the future, and I hope that other managers will learn that there is still a place for an out-and-out winger. And I might add that even the great wingers like Alan Morton, Bobby Ferrier and Sandy Archibald probably only played for about 20 or 30 minutes in any game, but as entertainers and match-winners they were invaluable.

But while I might seem to be girning here about the quality and the type of game we are now being asked to watch, I'll still watch it! It is still the greatest game on earth, and don't we fans know it.

The players are very much actors in studded boots. They love the roar of the crowd, just as I did in those far-off years. But in those far-off years I always tried to earn my applause.

I would try and be last man out when Rangers took the field on a Saturday. The crowd would cheer you on to the field. I always felt that I shouldn't be cheered until I had done something. Until I had earned it. It might have been some kind of superstition I suppose, or some strange quirk in my make-up.

But I did feel that I wanted to work for my applause. A good goal, a good pass or a good tackle. As a player I respected my profession and I think the fans of Airdrie and Rangers, in particular, recognised this. I have nothing but good memories from my career.

And most of them are in this book.

Appendix 1

Major Matches

Bob McPhail played in 31 major games during his career from 1923 to 1941. He played 17 times for Scotland, all of them at inside-left, and six times for the Scottish League, in the same position.

He played in eight Scottish Cup finals — once with Airdrie and seven times for Rangers. He was a loser on only one occasion, the 1929 final, when Kilmarnock won 2-0.

Here are the teams he played in. The names read like a *Who's Who* of the greatest players in Scottish football before the war:

THE INTERNATIONALS

Against England
2 April 1927, at Hampden Park: Score: Scotland 1 England 2.
J Harkness (Queen's Park); W McStay (Celtic, captain), R Thomson (Falkirk); T Morrison (St Mirren), J Gibson (Partick Thistle), J McMullan (Manchester City); A McLean (Celtic), A Cunningham (Rangers), H Gallacher (Newcastle United), R McPhail (Airdrie), A Morton (Rangers).
Attendance: 111,214.
Scorer: Alan Morton.

28 March 1931, at Hampden Park: Score: Scotland 2 England 0.
J Thomson (Celtic); D Blair (Clyde), J Nibloe (Kilmarnock); C McNab (Dundee), D Meiklejohn (Rangers, captain), J Miller (St Mirren); S Archibald (Rangers), G Stevenson (Motherwell), J McGrory (Celtic), R McPhail (Rangers), A Morton (Rangers).
Attendance: 129,810.
Scorers: George Stevenson, Jimmy McGrory.

1 April 1933, at Hampden Park: Score: Scotland 2 England 1.
J Jackson (Partick Thistle); A Anderson (Hearts), W McGonagle (Celtic); P Wilson (Celtic), R Gillespie (Queen's Park, captain). G Brown (Rangers); J Crawford (Queen's Park), J Marshall (Rangers), J McGrory (Celtic), R McPhail (Rangers), D Duncan (Derby County).
Attendance: 134,710
Scorer: Jimmy McGrory (2).

6 April 1935, at Hampden Park: Score: Scotland 2 England 0.
J Jackson (Chelsea); A Anderson (Hearts), G Cummings (Partick Thistle); A Massie (Hearts) J Simpson (Rangers, captain), G Brown (Rangers); C Napier (Celtic), T Walker (Hearts), H Gallacher (Derby County), R McPhail (Rangers), D Duncan (Derby County).
Attendance: 129,693.
Scorer: Dally Duncan (2).

17 April 1937, at Hampden Park. Score: Scotland 3 England 1.
J Dawson (Rangers); A Anderson (Hearts), A Beattie (Preston North End); A Massie (Hearts), J Simpson (Rangers, captain), G Brown (Rangers); J Delaney (Celtic), T Walker (Hearts), F O'Donnell (Preston North End), R McPhail (Rangers), D Duncan (Derby County).
Attendance: 149,547 (all-time record for British football).
Scorers: Bob McPhail (2), Frank O'Donnell.

Against Northern Ireland

21 February 1931, at Windsor Park Belfast. Score: Scotland 0 N Ireland 0.
J Thomson (Celtic); J Crapnell (Airdrie), J Nibloe (Kilmarnock); P Wilson (Celtic), G Walker (St Mirren), F Hill (Aberdeen); J Murdoch (Motherwell), P Scarff (Celtic), B Yorston (Aberdeen), R McPhail (Rangers), A Morton (Rangers, captain).
Attendance: 20,000.

19 September 1931, at Ibrox Stadium. Score: Scotland 3 N Ireland 1.
R Hepburn (Ayr United); D Blair (Clyde), R McAulay (Rangers); A Massie (Hearts), D Meiklejohn (Rangers, captain), G Brown (Rangers); J Crawford (Queen's Park), G Stevenson (Motherwell), J McGrory (Celtic), R McPhail (Rangers), J Connor (Sunderland).
Attendance: 40,000.
Scorers: George Stevenson, Jimmy McGrory and Bob McPhail.

19 September 1932, at Windsor Park, Belfast. Score: Scotland 4 N Ireland 0.
A McLaren (St Johnstone); D Gray (Rangers), J Crapnell (Airdrie, captain); A Massie (Hearts), J Johnstone (Hearts), W Telfer (Motherwell); J Crawford (Queen's Park), G Stevenson (Motherwell), J McGrory (Celtic), R McPhail (Rangers), J King (Hamilton Accies).
Attendance: 40,000.
Scorers: Bob McPhail (2), Jimmy McGrory, Jamie King.

16 September 1933, at Celtic Park. Score: Scotland 1 N Ireland 2.
J Harkness (Hearts); A Anderson (Hearts), W McGonagle (Celtic, captain); A Massie (Hearts), A Low (Falkirk), W Telfer (Motherwell); J Boyd (Newcastle United), A Venters (Rangers), J McGrory (Celtic), R McPhail (Rangers), J King (Hamilton Accies).
Attendance: 27,135.
Scorer: Bob McPhail.

10 November 1937, at Pittodrie Stadium, Aberdeen. Score: Scotland 1 N Ireland 1.
J Dawson (Rangers); A Anderson (Hearts), G Cummings (Aston Villa); D McKenzie (Brentford), J Simpson (Rangers, captain), A Hastings, (Sunderland); J Delaney (Celtic), T Walker (Hearts), J Smith (Rangers), R McPhail (Rangers), R Reid (Brentford).
Attendance: 21,878.
Scorer: Jimmy Smith.

Against Wales

27 October 1928, at Ibrox Stadium. Score: Scotland 4 Wales 2.
J Harkness (Hearts); D Gray (Rangers), D Blair (Clyde); T Muirhead (Rangers), W S King (Queen's Park), J McMullan (Manchester City, captain); A Jackson (Huddersfield Town), J Dunn (Everton), H Gallacher (Newcastle United), R McPhail (Rangers), A Morton (Rangers).
Attendance: 55,000.
Scorers: Hughie Gallacher (3), Jimmy Dunn.

31 October 1931, at Racecourse Ground, Wrexham. Score: Scotland 3 Wales 2.
J Harkness (Hearts); D Blair (Clyde), R McAulay (Rangers); A Massie

(Hearts), D Meiklejohn (Rangers, captain), G Brown (Rangers); R Thomson (Celtic), G Stevenson (Motherwell), J McGrory (Celtic), R McPhail (Rangers), A Morton (Rangers).
Attendance: 10,860.
Scorers: George Stevenson, Bertie Thomson, Bob McPhail.

30 October 1937, at Ninian Park, Cardiff. Score: Scotland 1 Wales 2.
J Dawson (Rangers); A Anderson (Hearts), G Cummings (Aston Villa); A Massie (Hearts), J Simpson (Rangers, captain), G Brown (Rangers); R Main (Rangers), T Walker (Hearts), F O'Donnell (Preston North End), R McPhail (Rangers), D Duncan (Derby County).
Attendance: 41,800.
Scorer: Alex Massie.

Against France

8 May 1932, in Colombes Stadium, Paris. Score: Scotland 3 France 1.
J Harkness (Hearts); J Crapnell (Airdrie), J Nibloe (Kilmarnock); A Massie (Hearts), R Gillespie (Queen's Park, captain), J Miller (St Mirren); J Crawford (Queen's Park), A Thomson (Celtic), N Dewar (Third Lanark), R McPhail (Rangers), A Morton (Rangers).
Attendance: 20,000
Scorer: Neilly Dewar (3).

Against Austria

29 November 1933, at Hampden Park. Score: Scotland 2 Austria 2.
J Kennaway (Celtic); A Anderson (Hearts), W McGonagle (Celtic); D Meiklejohn (Rangers, captain), P Watson (Blackpool), G Brown (Rangers); D Ogilvie (Motherwell), R Bruce (Middlesbrough), W McFadyen (Motherwell), R McPhail (Rangers), D Duncan (Derby County).
Attendance: 62,000.
Scorers: Davie Meiklejohn and Willie McFadyen.

Against Germany

14 October 1936, at Hampden Park. Score: Scotland 2 Germany 0.
J Dawson (Rangers); A Anderson (Hearts), G Cummings (Aston

Villa); A Massie (Hearts), J Simpson (Rangers, captain), G Brown (Rangers); J Delaney (Celtic), T Walker (Hearts), M Armstrong (Aberdeen), R McPhail (Rangers), D Duncan (Derby County).
Attendance: 50,000.
Scorer: Jimmy Delaney (2).

Against Czechoslovakia

22 May 1937, in Prague. Score: Scotland 3 Czechoslovakia 1.
J Dawson (Rangers), R Hogg (Celtic), A Beattie (Preston North End); C Thomson (Sunderland), J Simpson (Rangers, captain), G Brown (Rangers); J Delaney (Celtic), T Walker (Hearts), F O'Donnell (Preston North End), R McPhail (Rangers), T Gillick (Everton).
Attendance: 35,000.
Scorers: Jimmy Simpson, Bob McPhail and Torry Gillick.

SCOTTISH LEAGUE HONOURS

Against English League

19 March 1927, at Filbert Street, Leicester. Score: Scottish League 2 English League 2.
T Ferguson (Falkirk); W McStay (Celtic), R Thomson (Falkirk); J Gibson (Partick Thistle), J McDougall (Airdrie), T Craig (Rangers); H Ritchie (Hibs), G Stevenson (Motherwell), J McGrory (Celtic), R McPhail (Airdrie), A Morton (Rangers).
Attendance: 26,000.
Scorers: Bob McPhail, Jimmy McGrory.

7 November 1931, at Celtic Park. Score: Scottish League 4 English League 3.
J Jackson (Partick Thistle); J Crapnell (Airdrie), W McGonagle (Celtic); D Meiklejohn (Rangers), J McStay (Celtic), G Brown (Rangers); R Thomson (Celtic), J McMenemy (Motherwell), J McGrory (Celtic), R McPhail (Rangers), A Morton (Rangers).
Attendance: 51,000.
Scorers: Jimmy McGrory (2), Bob McPhail, Willie "Peter" McGonagle (pen).

9 November 1932, at Maine Road, Manchester. Score: Scottish League 3 English League 0.
J Jackson (Partick Thistle); J Crapnell (Airdrie), W McGonagle (Celtic); D Meiklejohn (Rangers), J Johnstone (Hearts), C Geatons (Celtic); S Archibald (Rangers), J Marshall (Rangers), N Dewar (Third Lanark), R McPhail (Rangers), C Napier (Celtic).
Attendance: 29,603.
Scorers: Charlie Napier (2), Neilly Dewar.

10 February 1934, at Ibrox Stadium. Score: Scottish League 2 English League 2.
J Kennaway (Celtic); A Anderson (Hearts), W McGonagle (Celtic); A Massie (Hearts), J Simpson (Rangers), G Brown (Rangers); R Main (Rangers), G Stevenson (Motherwell), J Fleming (Rangers), R McPhail (Rangers), W G Nicholson (Rangers).
Attendance: 59,000.
Scorers: Jimmy Simpson and Bob McPhail.

21 October 1936, at Goodison Park, Liverpool. Score: Scottish League 0 English League 2.
J Dawson (Rangers); A Anderson (Hearts), J Shaw (Airdrie); C Geatons (Celtic), T Smith (Kilmarnock), G Brown (Rangers); J Delaney (Celtic), T Walker (Hearts), M Armstrong (Aberdeen), R McPhail (Rangers), D Kinnear (Rangers).
Attendance: 25,000.

Against Irish League

27 October 1926, at Tynecastle Park. Score: Scottish League 5 Irish League 2.
A McClory (Motherwell); T Reid (Hearts), W Wiseman (Queen's Park); P Kerr (Hearts), J Rankine (Dundee), T Craig (Rangers); P Connolly (Celtic), J White (Hearts), J McGrory (Celtic), R McPhail (Airdrie), W Cook (Dundee).
Attendance: 6,700.
Scorers: Bob McPhail (2), John White (2) and Jimmy McGrory.

Bob McPhail's
Eight Scottish Cup Final Appearances

Airdrie 2 Hibs 0, *1924, at Ibrox Stadium.*
Airdrie: Ewart; Dick, McQueen; Preston, McDougall, Bennie; Reid, Russell, Gallacher, McPhail, Sommerville.
Attendance: 59,218.
Scorer: Willie Russell (2).

Rangers 4 Celtic 0, *1928, at Hampden Park.*
Rangers: T Hamilton; Gray, R Hamilton; Buchanan, Meiklejohn, Craig; Archibald, Cunningham, Fleming, McPhail, Morton.
Attendance: 118,115.
Scorers: Davie Meiklejohn (pen), Bob McPhail, Sandy Archibald (2).

Rangers 0 Kilmarnock 2, *1929, at Hampden Park.*
Rangers: T Hamilton; Gray, R Hamilton; Buchanan, Meiklejohn, Craig; Archibald, Muirhead, Fleming, McPhail, Morton.
Attendance: 114,708.

Rangers 2 Partick Thistle 1 (after 0-0 draw), *1930, at Hampden Park.*
Rangers: T Hamilton; Gray, R Hamilton; McDonald, Meiklejohn, Craig; Archibald, Marshall, Fleming, McPhail, Morton.
Attendance: 103,686.
Scorers: Jimmy (Doc) Marshall and Tully Craig.

Rangers 3 Kilmarnock 0 (after 1-1 draw), *1932, at Hampden Park.*
Rangers: T Hamilton; Gray, McAulay; Meiklejohn, Simpson, Brown; Archibald, Marshall, English, McPhail, Fleming.
Attendance: 104,695.
Scorers: Jimmy Fleming, Bob McPhail and Sam English.

Rangers 5 St Mirren 0, 1934, at Hampden Park.
Rangers: T Hamilton; Gray, McDonald; Meiklejohn, Simpson, Brown; Main, Marshall, Smith, McPhail and Nicholson.
Attendance: 113,403.
Scorers: Willie Nicholson (2), Bob McPhail, Bobby Main and Jimmy Smith.

Rangers 2 Hamilton Accies 1, *1935, at Hampden Park.*
Rangers: Dawson; Gray, McDonald; Kennedy, Simpson, Brown; Main, Venters, Smith, McPhail, Gillick.
Attendance: 87,285.
Scorer: Jimmy Smith (2).

Rangers 1 Third Lanark 0, *1936 at Hampden Park.*
Rangers: Dawson; Gray, Cheyne; Meiklejohn, Simpson, Brown; Fiddes, Venters, Smith, McPhail, Turnbull.
Attendance: 88,859.
Scorer: Bob McPhail.

Appendix 2

The McPhail Goals

In his 12 full seasons with Rangers, until the outbreak of the Second World War, Bob McPhail scored 236 league goals, which is still an Ibrox club record.

His 70 goals in 106 league games for Airdrie gives him a career total of 306 goals which has been beaten in Scotland by only one player — Jimmy McGrory of Celtic.

McGrory, who formed a lethal scoring partnership with McPhail for Scotland and the Scottish League, scored 13 goals for Clydebank and 397 goals for Celtic in league football, for a record total of 410 goals in 408 games, a phenomenal record which will surely never be beaten.

Bob's overall scoring total with Airdrie and Rangers is 355 in league and Cup football, which is remarkable, considering he was the old-style fetch-and-carry inside-forward, who was expected to help his defenders when required.

Here is the complete career statistics of Bob McPhail in detail:

	Season	League Games	League Goals	Cup Ties	Cup Goals
AIRDRIE	1923-24	6	1	3	0
	1924-25	33	12	3	1
	1925-26	36	24	5	1
	1926-27	31	33	3	1
	Total	106	70	14	3
RANGERS	1926-27	—	—	3	4
	1927-28	35	17	10	8
	1928-29	34	18	7	3
	1929-30	23	19	12	0
	1930-31	34	20	7	3
	1931-32	35	22	14	7
	1932-33	31	30	7	3
	1933-34	25	22	10	3
	1934-35	30	14	11	1
	1935-36	26	23	10	5
	1936-37	33	26	5	5
	1937-38	25	10	7	3
	1938-39	23	15	4	0
	Total	354	236	107	45
	Aggregate Total	460	306	121	49

Note: Bob played five wartime Regional League games for Rangers and scored twice in season 1939-40. In season 1940-41 he played 13 games for St Mirren in the Southern League and scored seven goals. All wartime games, however, are unofficial.

The Ibrox Chart of Bob McPhail's Consistency

The remarkable consistency of Bob McPhail as a scorer in his 12 seasons with Rangers is shown in this chart of the club's top three league scorers from 1927 to 1939. Only once was Bob out of the top three and that was in season 1937-38 when he made only 25 league appearances because of injury and scored 10 goals — two behind second place Alex Venters and Davie Kinnear.

Leading scorers were:

1927-28 (Champions) — 1. J. Fleming 35. 2. R. McPhail 17 and S. Archibald 17.

1928-29 (Champions) — 1. J. Fleming 33. 2. R. McPhail 18. 3. A. Morton 15.

1929-30 (Champions) — 1. J. Fleming 27. 2. R. McPhail 19. 3. J. Marshall 14.

1930-31 (Champions) — 1. J. Smith 22. 2. R. McPhail 20 and J. Marshall 20.

1931-32 (Runners-up) 1. S. English 44. R. McPhail 22. 3. J. Fleming 16.

1932-33 (Champions) — 1. J. Smith 33. 2. R. McPhail 30. 3. J. Marshall 15.

1933-34 (Champions) — 1. J. Smith 41. 2. R. McPhail 22. 3. J. Fleming 16.

1934-35 (Champions) — 1. J. Smith 36. 2. T. Gillick 17. 3. R. McPhail 14.

1935-36 (Runners-up) — 1. J. Smith 31. 2 R. McPhail 23. 3. A. Venters 17.

1936-37 (Champions) — 1. J. Smith 30. 2. R. McPhail 26. 3. A. Venters 10.

1937-38 (Third) — 1. J. Smith 22. 2. A. Venters 12 and D. Kinnear 12.
1938-39 (Champions) — 1. A. Venters 35. 2. W. Thornton 23. 3. R. McPhail 15.

A Rangers director R G "Bob" Campbell offered to give Bob a golf ball every time he scored a goal with his left foot during a certain season. Says Bob: "I managed to score one or two, though this was normally the foot I used for standing on. But on one occasion I won a ball on default. I took a swipe at a ball with my right foot, missed it, and it hit my left foot and finished in the net."

Bob McPhail scored Rangers' 3,000th League goal against Cowdenbeath on 20 December, 1930, at Ibrox in a 7-0 victory.